Ed's GREATEST SINGALONG SONGS EVER

Sing along with Ed

ALPHABETICAL LISTING IN BACK

TITLE	PAGE
NICE MELODIES	**10**
House of the Rising Sun	11
City of New Orleans	12
Morning has Broken	13
Those were the Days my Friend	14
Scarborough Fair	15
Sound of Silence	16
Green Fields	17
Greensleeves	18
Love is Blue	19
Green Green	20
Five Hundred Miles	21
Delilah	22
Four Strong Winds	23
Puff the Magic Dragon	24
Where have all the flowers Gone	25
Ghost Riders	26
Country Roads	27
Annies Song	28
Hava Nagilh	29
Old Toy trains	30
Cotton Fields Back Home	31
Wildwood Flower	32
Yellow Bird	33
Never On Sunday	34
I Don't Have a Wooden Heart	35
All I have to Do is Dream	36
The Singing Nun	37
Eidleweiss	38
Who's Sorry Now	39
Cecilia	41
Ob La Di	42
Never Ending Song of Love	43
Kalinka	44
Guantanamera	45

I'll See You in my Dreams	46
MARTY ROBBINS	**47**
El Paso	48
Big Iron	49
Running Gun	50
The Hanging Tree	51
Devil Woman	52
JOHN DENVER	**53**
Country Roads	54
Annie's Song	55
For Baby	56
Good to be back Home Again	57
Green Green Grass of Home	58
Calypso	59
Thank God I'm a Country Boy	60
Grammas Feather Bed	61
The Night They Drove old Dixie	62
ABBA	**63**
I Have A dream	64
Take A Chance On Me	65
Eagle	67
The Piper	68
BOB DYLAN	**69**
Blowin In The Wind	70
Don't Think Twice	71
Mr Tamborine Man	72
Times They are A Changin	73
It Ai'nt Me Babe	74
A Hard Rains Gonna Fall	75
Gotta Travel On	76
ROGER WHITTACKER	**77**
Love Is Blue	78
Durham Town	79
New World In the Morning	80
The Last Farwell	81
River Lady	82
IRISH MELODIES	**83**

Cockles and Mussels	84
Danny Boy	85
Star Of The County Down	86
Whiskey In The Jar	87
There is a Tavern in this Town	88
Wild Colonial Boy	89
The Unicorn Song	90
BONEY M	**91**
Rasputin	92
Rivers Of Babylon	93
Brown Girl In The Ring	94
NEIL DIAMOND	**95**
Song Sung Blue	96
Sweet Caroline	97
Craklin Rosie	98
KENNY ROGERS	**99**
The Gambler	100
Lucille	102
Rueben James	103
JOHNNY CASH	**104**
Big River	105
Boy Named Sue	106
Home Of The Blues	107
Ballad Of A Teenage Queen	108
Five Feet High and Risen	109
Get Rhythm	112
Guess Things Happen That Way	113
Tennessee Stud	114
Ring Of Fire	115
Folsom Prison Blues	116
Tennessee Flat Top Box	117
Daddy Sang Bass	118
I Walk The Line	119
WESTERN COUNTRY MIX	**120**
Abilene	121
Act Naturally	122
Amanda	123

On The Road Again	124
Have I Told You Lately That I Love You	125
Heart Aches by the Number	126
Jambalaya	127
Kiss An Angel Good Morning	128
Luckenbach Texas	129
Don`t Take Your Love To Town	130
Oakie From Muskogee	131
Bobby McGee	132
King Of The Road	133
Sixteen Tons	134
OH Lord It's Hard to Be Humble	135
Put Another Log On The Fire	136
Sundown	137
Shenandoah	138
Storms Never Last	139
Just An Old Hippy	140
Let Me Be There	141
Rhinestone Cowboy	142
Walk On By	143
Summer Wages	144
Della And The Dealer	145
Wolverton Mountain	146
It`s A Heartache	148
Silver Threads And Golden Needles	149
Three wheels On My Wagon	151
Black Fly	152
Joy To The world	153
CARIBBEAN BEAT	**154**
Sloop John B	155
Jamaica Farewell	156
La Bamba	157
Marianne	158
I Wanna Go Home	159
Farewell Adelita	160
KINGSTON TRIO	**161**
Tom Dooley	162
The MTA	163

Greenback Dollar	164
Rueben James	165
Tijuana Jail	166
A Worried Man	167
Everglades	168
El Matador	169
Coplas Revisited	170
Hi Lili Lili Lo	171
Raspberries Strawberries	172
Sinking Of The Reuben James	173
Roving Gambler	174
The Erie Canal	175
Blow Ye winds	176
I`d Like To Teach The world To Sing	177
Drunken Sailor	178
LEONARD COHEN	**179**
The Future	180
Take This Waltz	181
Closing Time	182
Everybody Knows	185
OLD FAVORITES	**186**
Jesse James	187
My Lover was a Logger (Logger Love)	188
Mrs. Robinson	189
Big Bad John	190
I Can See Clearly	191
England Swings	192
Running Bear	193
Squaws Along The Yukon	194
Wings Of A Dove	195
Froggie went A Courtin	196
Bottle Of Wine	197
Frankie And Johny	198
Just walking In The Rain	199
Heartbreak Hotel	200
The Battle Of New Orleans	201
Wabash Cannonball	202

Michael Row The Boat Ashore	203
Jackson	204
Cool Water	205
Cry Of The wild Goose	206
The Reverend Mr Black	207
Hakuna Matata	208
The Happy Wanderer	210
If I Were A Rich Man	211
Vaya Codios	213
Oh My Darling Clemintine	214
Grandfathers Clock	215
When The Saints Go Marchin In	216
Lemon Tree	217
This Land Is Your Land	218
Are You Lonesome Tonight	219
Waltzing Matilda	220
Stewball	221
Walk Right In	222
North To Alaska	223
Delta Dawn	224
Margaritaville	225
Watermelon Wine	226
Sneaky Snake	227
I Like Beer	228
Thunder Road	229
Fast Freight	230
Raindrops Keep Falling On My Head	231
Mellow Yellow	232
High Hopes	233
DONOVAN	**235**
Jennifer Juniper	236
Universal Soldier	237
Colors	239
Hurdy Gurdy Man	240
OLD FUNNIES	**241**
Monster Mash	242
Alley Opp	243
Purple People Eater	244

Witch Doctor	245
Itsy Bitsy Bikini	246
Tie Me Kangaroo Down Sport	247
ROCKIN & ROLLIN	**248**
Sweet Georgia Brown	249
Book Of Love	250
Party Doll	251
Down By The Station	252
Kisses Sweeter Than Wine	253
Singin The Blues	254
Bad Bad Leroy Brown	255
Honeycomb	256
All I Have o Do Is Dream	257
Bye Bye Love	258
Be Bop A Lula	259
I Kissed Ya	260
Jonny Is A Joker	261
Wake Up Little Susie	262
Young Love	263
Young Love 2	264
Its So Easy	265
Peggy Sue	266
Rave On	267
That`ll Be The Day	268
Well Alright	269
Blue Suede Shoes	270
Chantilly Lace	271
White Lightening	272
Hound Dog	273
Singing The Blues	274
Jailhouse Rock	275
Johny B Goode	276
Love Potion Number 9	277
Only The Lonely	278
Book Of Love	279
Save The Last Dance For Me	280
All American Boy	281
Try To Remember	283

Downtown	284
Look what They`ve Done To My Song	285
Kokomo	286
Taken`Care Of Business	287
American Pie	288
XMAS FAVORITES	**289**
God Rest ye Merry Gentelmen	290
Good King Wenseslas	291
Hark the Herald Angels Sing	292
Have Yourself a Merry Little Christmas	293
It Came Upon a Midnight Clear	294
Here Comes Santa Claus	295
Its Beginning to look a lot like Xmas	296
Jingle Bells	297
Jingle Bell Rock	298
Jolly old St Nicolas	299
Joy to the World	300
O come all Ye Faithfull	301
O Holy night	302
Rudolf the red nosed reindeer	303
Santa claus is coming to town	304
Silent Night	305
Silver Bells	306
Six White Boomers	307
The First Noel	308
The Little Drummer Boy	309
Twelve Days of Xmas	310
We Three Kings of Orient are	314
We Wish you a Merry Christmas	315
White Christmas	316
The Christmas Song	317
Sleighride	318
Rockin Around the Christmas Tree	319
O Little Town of Bethlehem	320
Frosty The Snowman	321

NICE MELODIES

HOUSE OF THE RISING SUN

    Am   C   D   F
There is a house in New Orleans
Am   C   E7
They call it the rising sun
Am   C   D   F
It has been the ruin of many poor girl
Am   E   M   C D F Am E Am E
And me, Oh Lord was one

If I had listened to what mama said, I'd be at home today
But being so young and foolish, poor girl
Let a gambler lead me astray

My mother is a tailor, She sews those new blue jeans
My sweetheart is a drunkard Lord, Drinks down in New Orleans

The only thing a drunkard needs, Is a suitcase and a trunk
The only time he's satisfied, Is when he's on a drunk

Go tell my baby sister, Never do like I have done
To shun that house in New Orleans They call the rising sun

He'll fill his glasses to the brim, he passes them around
And the only pleasure he gets out of life is bumming around the town
Its one foot on the platform And the other one on the train
I'm going back to New Orleans To wear the all and chain

I'm going back to New Orleans, my race is almost run
I'm going back to spend my life beneath that rising sun
Etc.
Dm7 000211
Dm6 000201

CITY OF NEW ORLEANS

G   D   G
Ridin on the City of New Or-leans
Em   C   G
Ilinois Central Monday morning rail
G   D   G
Fifteen cars and fifteen restless riders,
      Em   D   G
Three conductors and twenty five sacks of mail
    Em
All along the south bound Odyssey,
  Bm
the train pulls out of Kankakee
  D   A
And rolls a long the houses, farms and fields
Em
Pass in' towns that have no name and freight
  Bm
And freight yard full of old black men
  D   D7   G
And grave yards….. of the rusted automobiles……….
C   D7   G
Good morning A mer i ca…… how are …..you?
Em   C   G
Don't you know I'm your native son
  G   D   Em
I'm the train they call the city of New Orleans
    C   D   G
I'll be gone five hundred miles when the day is done

Dealin card games with the old men in the club car
Penny a point ain't no one keepn' score
Pass the paper bag that holds the bottle
Feel the wheels grumbling neath the floor
And the sons of Pulman porters, and the sons of engineers
Ride their fathers magic carpet made of steel
Mothers with their babies asleep are rockin' to the gentle beat

MORNING HAS BROKEN

INTRO   G   A F   Bm   G7   C   F   C

C   C   Dm   G   F   C
Morning has broken,   like the first morning
C   Em   Am   Dsus   D   G
Blackbird has spoken,   like the first bird
C   F   C   Am   D
Praise for the singing, Praise for the morning
G   C   F   G7   C   F
Praise for them springing fresh from the world
INSERT   F   G   E   Am   G   C   G7
  Am   F#   Bm   G   D   A7/D   D

Sweet the rains new fall, sun lit from heaven
Like the first dew fall on the first grass
Praise for the sweetness of the wet garden.
Sprung in completeness where his feet pass

D   Em   A   G   D
Mine is the sunlight, Mine is the morning
D   F#m   Bm   E7   A
Born of the one light Eden saw play
D   G   D   Bm   E
Praise with elation, Praise every morning
A   D   G   A7   D
God's recreation of the new day
INSERT G   A   F#   Bm   G7   C   C   F   D
  Am   F#   Bm   G   D   A7.D   D

THOSE WERE THE DAYS

<pre>
Am   Am6   Am7   Am6
Once upon a time there was a tavern,
A   Dm   Dm6
Where we used to raise a glass or two
  Dm   Am7   Am6
Remember how we laughed away the hours.
   B   B9   E
And dreamed of all the great things we could do
</pre>
CHORUS
<pre>
           Am   Dm
Those were the days my friend, We thought they'd never end,
           G   G7   C
We'd sing and dance forever and a day
           Dm   Am
We'd live the life we choose, we'd fight and never loose
          E7   Am
For we were young and sure to have our way
             A   Dm
La la la la   la la   la la la la   la la
          F7   E7   Am
Those were the days Oh yes those were the days
</pre>

Then the busy years went rushing by us,
We lost our starry notions on the way
If by chance I'd see you in the tavern
We'd smile at one an other and we'd say
CHORUS
Just tonight I stood before the tavern,
Nothing seemed the way it used to be
In the glass I saw a strange reflection
Was that lonely fellow really me?
CHORUS
Through the door there came familiar laughter
 I saw your face and heard you call my name
Oh my friends we're older but no wiser
For in our hearts the dreams are still the same

SCARBOROUGH FAIR

```
   Dm              C           Dm      F
Are you going to Scarborouh Fair
        Dm      G         Dm
Parsley, sage, rosemary and thyme
   Bb      F              C
Remember me to one who lives there
       Dm     C              Dm
For once she was a true love of mine
Dm              C          Dm     F
Have her make me a cambrie shirt
        Dm      G         Dm
Parsley, sage, rosemary and thyme
   Bb      F              C
Without a seam or gfine needle to work
       Dm     C              Dm
And then she'll be a true love of mine
 Dm             C          Dm    F
Have he wash it in yonder dry well
    Dm          G          Dm
Parsley sage, rosemary and thyme
        Bb      F              C
Where never a drop of water ever fell
       Dm     C              Dm
And then shell be a true love of mine
Dm              C        Dm    F
If she tells me she cant I'll reply
          Dm     G        Dm
Parsley sage, rosemary and thyme
Bb       F                     C
Let me know that at least she will try
    Dm     C               Dm
And she'll be  atrue love of mine
```

SOUND OF SILENCE
(Paul Simon)

Am   G
Hello darkness my old friend
                         Am
I've come to talk with you again
C   F   C
Because a vision softly creeping
                 F   C
Left its seeds while I was sleeping
     F   C
And he vision that was planted in my brain
     Am
Still remains
C   G   Am
Within the sound of silence

In restless dreams I walk alone
Narrow streets with cobbled stones
Neath the halo of a street lamp
I've turned my collar to the cold and damp
When my eyes were stabbed by the flash of a neon light
Split the night
And touched the sound of silence

And in the naked light I saw
Ten thousand people maybe more
People talking without speaking
People hearing without listening
People writing songs that voices never hear
And no one does
Disturb the sound of Silence

GREEN FIELDS

Am	Dm	Am	E7

Once there were green fields kissed by the sun

Am	Dm	Am	E7

Once there were valleys where rivers used to run

F	G7	C	Am

Once there were blue skys with white clouds high above

F	G7	C	E7

Once they were part of an everlasting love

Am	D7	Am	E	Am

We were lovers who strolled through green fields

DITTO CHORDS

Green fields are gone now, Parched by the sun
Gone from the valleys where rivers used to run
Gone with the cold wind that sweps in to my heart
Gone with the lovers who let their dreams depart
Where are the greenfields that we used to roam

I'll never know what made you run a way
How can I keep searching when dark clouds hide the day
I only know there nothing here for me
Nothing in this wide world left for me to see
But I'll keep on waitin til you return

I'll keep on waiting until the day you learn
You can't be happy while your hearts on the roam
You can't e happy until you bring it home
Home to the greenfilds and me once again
Home to the greenfilds and me once again

GREEN SLEEVES

Em   D
Alas my love you do me wrong
 C   B7
To cast me out discourteously
    Em   D
And I have loved you so long
   B7   Em
Delighting in your company
CHORUS
G   D
Green sleeves was all my joy
C   B7
Green sleeves was my delight
G   D
Green sleeves was my heart of gold,
C   B7   Em
And who but lady Green Sleeves

I have been ready at your hand
To grant what ever you could crave,
I have both waged life and land
Your love and good will for to have
CHORUS

I brought three kerchers to thy head
That were brought fine and gallantly
I kept thee both board and bread
Which cost my purse well favourably
CHORUS

LOVE IS BLUE

|Am D   Am D|
|Am   D   G   Am   C|
Blue blue, my world is blue, blue is my world
| G   Am|
Now I'm without you
|Am   D   G   Am   C|
Grey, grey my life is grey, Cold is my heart
| E   Am|
since you went away
|C   F C   F   C|
When we met how the bright sun shone
|Dm   F   G7|
Then love died now the rainbow is gone
|Am   D   G   G|
Black, black the nights I've known
|Am   C   D   Am|
Longing for you so lost and alone

Gone gone the love we knew
Blue is my world now I'm without you
Red, red, my eyes are red
Crying for you alone in my bed
Green green, my jealous heart
I doubted you and now were apart

When we met how the bright sun shone
Then love died now the rainbow is gone
Black, black the nights I've known
Longing for you so lost and alone
Blue blue, my world is blue
Blue is my world, I'm without you

GREEN GREEN
(Barry McGuire)

```
G                C                    G            D7
Green Green it's green they say on the far side of the hill
G                C    G                        D7       G
Green, green, I'm goin away to where the grass is greener
still
         G      Bm       C        G
Well I told my mamma the day I was born
           C           D7        G
"Don cha cry when you see I'm gone
            Bm          C         G        C
You know there aint no woman gonna settle me down,
    D7              G
I just gotta keep travelin on Singin…
```
CHORUS
```
G                C                    G            D7
```
Green Green it's green they say on the far side of the hill
```
G                C                    G    D7       G
```
Green, green, I'm goin away to where the grass is greener still

No there ain't no body in this whole wide world
Gonna tell me how to spend my time
I'm just a good lovin' ramble-in man,
Say buddy can you spare me a dime
Hear me cryin'…
CHORUS

I don't care when the sun goes down,
where I lay my weary head
Green, green valley or a rocky road,
it's there I'm gonna make my bed
CHORUS

FIVE HUNDRED MILES

G   Em C   Am
If you miss the train I'm on you will know that I am gone
   D7 Am7 D7 C G   C G
You can hear the whistle blow a hundred miles
    G   Em
A hundred miles, a hundred miles,
 C   Am
a hundred miles, a hundred miles,
   D7 Am7 D7 C G
You can hear the whistle blow a hundred miles

Lord, I'm one, lord I'm two, Lord I'm three, Lord I'm four,
Lord, I'm five hundred miles away from home
Away from home, away from home,
away from home away from home
Lord I'm five hundred miles away from home

Not a shirt on my back, not a penny to my name,
Lord I can't go back home this a way
This away, this a way, this a way, this a way
Lord I cant go back home this a way.

Am7 002213

DELILAH

```
     Em                                  B7
I saw the light on the night that I passed by her window
     Em                              B7
I saw the flickering shadows of Love on her blind
 E      E7       Am
She was my woman
     Em             B7                    Em
D7
As she deceived me I watched and went out of my mind
 G          D7
My my my Delilah
             F#  G
Why, why, why Delilah
 G   D7  G  G7      C                  A7
I could see   that girl was no good for me
 G             D7              G         B7
But I was lost like a slave that no man could free
 Em
Forgive me Delilah,
   B7              Em
I just couldn't take any more
```

At break of day when the man drove away I was waiting,
I crossed the street to her house and she opened the door
She stood there laughing
I felt the knife in my hand and she laughed no more
My my my Delilah
Why, why, why Delilah
So before they come to break down the door
Forgive me Delilah
I just couldn't take any more

FOUR STRONG WINDS

G   Am   D   G
Four strong winds that blow lonely seven seas that run high
                  Am   D
All those things that don't change come what may
    G   Am
But the good times are all gone
    D   G
And I bound for moving on
    Am   C   D
I'll look for you if I'm ever back this way
       G   Am   D   G
I think I'll go out to Alberta, weathers good there in the fall
                       Am   D
Iv'e got some friends that I can go to working for
    G   Am   D   G
Still I wish you'd change your mind if I ask you one more time
       Am   C   D
But we've been through that a hundred times or more

If you get there before the snow flies and things are looking good
You can meet me if I send you down the fare
By then it will be winter not too much for you to do
Those winds sure blow cold away out there

PUFF THE MAGIC DRAGON

C   Em   C
Puff the magic dragon lived by the sea
         F   C   Am   D7   G
And frolicked in the autumn mist in a land called Honalee
C   Em   F   C
Little Jackie paper loved that rascal Puff
    F   C   Am
And brought him strings and sealing wax
D7   G   C   G
and other fancy stuff, Oh

Puff the magic dragon lived by the sea
And frolicked in the autumn mist in a land called Hon al lee
Puff the magic dragon lived by the sea
And frolicked in the autumn mist in a land called Hon al lee

Together they would travel on a boat with billowed sale
Jackie kept a look out perched on Puffs gigantic tail
Noble Kings and princes would bow when ever they came
Pirate ships would lower their flag when Puff roared out his name

A dragon lives forever but not so little boys
Painted wings and giant rings make way for other toys
One grey night it happened, Jackie Paper came no more
And Puff the mighty dragon he ceased his fearless roar

His head was bent in sorrow, green scales fell like rain
Puff no longer wet to play along the cherry lane
Without his life long friend, Puff could not be brave
So Puff the mighty dragon sadly slipped into his cave

WHERE HAVE ALL THE FLOWERS GONE
(Pete Seeger)

```
C                                         D7     G7
Where have all the flowers gone? Long time passing
C                               F          G
Where have all the Flowers gone? Long time ago
C
Where have all the flowers gone
                              G7
The girls have picked them every one
F       G7         C    F       G7          C
Oh when will they ever learn Oh when will they ever
learn?
```

Where have all the young girls gone? Long time passing
Where have all the young girls gone? Long time ago
Where have all the young girls gone
They've taken husbands every one
Oh when will they ever learn
Oh when will they ever learn?

Where have all the young men gone? Long time passing
Where have all the young men gone? Long time ago
Where have all the young men gone
They're all in uniform
Oh when will they ever learn
Oh when will they ever learn?

GHOST RIDERS
(Stan Jones)

Am   C   G
An old cowpoke went riding out One dark and windy day,
 AM   C   Am
Upon a ridge he rested as He went along his way,
When all at once a mighty herd Of red eyed cows he saw,
 F   Am
A-plowin' through the ragged skies And up a cloudy draw.
CHORUS
 Am   F   Am
Yippee-yi-ya, yippee-yi-yo, Ghost herd in the sky.

Their brands were still on fire and Their hooves were made of steel,
Their horns were black and shiny and Their hot breath he could feel,
A bolt of fear shot through him as He looked up in the sky,
For he saw the riders comin' hard And he heard their mournful cry:
CHORUS

Their faces gaunt, their eyes were blurred,
Their shirts all soaked with sweat,
They're riding hard to catch that herd, But they ain't caught 'em yet,
'cause they've got to ride forever on That range up in the sky,
On horses snortin' fire, as They ride on hear their cry:
CHORUS

The cowpokes loped on past him and He heard one call his name,
If you want to save your soul from hell A-riding on our range,
Then, cowboy, change your ways today, Or with us you will ride,
A-trying to catch the devil's herd Across these endless skies.
CHORUS

COUNTRY ROADS
(John Denver)

C   Am
Almost heaven West Virginia
G   F   C
Blue Ridge Mountains, Shenandoah River
                  Am
Life is old there, older than the trees,
G   F   C
Younger than the mountains, growin like a breeze
CHORUS
C   G   Am   F
Country roads, take me home, to the place I belong
    C   G   F   C
West Virginia, mountain momma, take me home, country roads
Am   G   C   Am
I hear her voice in the morning hour she calls me,
  F   C   G
The radio reminds of my home far away
   Am   G Bb   F
And driven' down the road I get a feelin that
  C   G7   F
I should have been home yesterday, yesterday,
CHORUS

C   Am
All my mem'ries gather round her,
G   F   C
Miners lady stranger to blue water
                Am
Dark and dusty painted on the sky
G   F   C
Misty taste of moonshine, tear drops in my eye
CHORUS

ANNIES SONG
John Denver

```
 G          C D  Em   C        G
```
You fill up my senses, like a night in the forest.
```
 G          C D    Am    C      D
```
Like a mountain in springtime, like a walk in the rain.
```
 G          C D     Em    C     G
```
Like a storm in the desert, like a sleepy blue ocean.
```
 G          C D   Am   D    G
```
You fill up my senses, come fill me again.
```
 G          C D   Em   C        G
```
Come let me love you, let me give my life for you.
```
 G          C D    Am   C      D
```
Let me drown in your laughter, let me die in your arms.
```
 G          C D    Em   C      G
```
Let me lay down beside you, let me always be with you.
```
 G       C D    Am   D    G
```
Come let me love you, come love me again.
HUM FIRST FIVE LINES

```
Em    C        G
```
Let me give my life to you
```
G          C D   Am   D    G
```
Come let me love you, Come love me again

```
 G          C D  Em   C        G
```
You fill up my senses, like a night in the forest.
```
 G          C  D   Am   C      D
```
Like a mountain in spring time, like a walk in the rain.
```
 G          C D    Em    C     G
```
Like a storm in the desert, like a sleepy blue ocean.
```
 G          C D   Am D    G
```
You fill up my senses, come fill me again.

HAVA NAGILAH

  E   Am   E
Hava nagila Hava nagila hava nagila vay nis mchayh
  E   Am   E
Hava nagila Hava nagila hava nagila vay nis mchayh
E   Dm
Hava nranenah, hava renanenah
                Em
Hava nerahnenah vay nis mchayh
E   Dm
Hava nranenah, hava renanenah
                        E7   Am
nerahnenah vay nis mchayh
               Am
Uru uruachim, Uru uruachim b'lev sameach,
              Am   Dm
Uruachim b'lev sameach, Uruachim blev sameach,
              Dm
Uruachim b lev sameach, Uruachim b lev sameach,
E   E7   Am
Uruachim! Uruachim! B'lev samach!

OLD TOY TRAINS
by: Roger Miller

```
D                         A7
Old toy trains little toy tracks
             G                  A7
Little toy drums coming from a  sack
            D             G
Carried  by a man dressed in white and red
            D         A7             D
Little boy don't you  think its  time you were in  bed
```

CHORUS
```
D         A7             G
Close your eyes, Listen to the  skies
     D       G
All  is  calm all is well
         A7            G           A7
Soon you'll  hear kris kringle  and the jingle bells
```

```
            D                 A7
Bringing  old toy  trains little toy  tracks
             G                  A7
Little toy drums coming from a  sack
            D             G
Carried by a  man dressed in white  and red
            D         A7            D
Little  boy don't you think its time you were in  bed
```

COTTON FIELDS BACK HOME

G
When I was a little bitty baby
                  C   G
My mama done rock me in the cradle
                            D
In them old cotton fields back home
      G   C   G
It was back in Louisiana, Just about a mile from Texarkana
        D   C
In them old cotton fields back home

Let me tell you now well got me in a fix
I caught a nail in my tire doing lickitey splits
I had to walk a long long way to town
Came upon a nice old man well he had a hat on
Wait a minute mister can you give me some directions
I gonna want to be right off for home

Don't care if them cotton balls get rotten
When I got you baby, who needs cotton
In them old cotton fields back home
Brother only one thing more that's gonna warm you
A summer's day out in California
It's gonna be those cotton fields back home

It was back in Louisiana, Just about a mile from Texarkana
Give me them cotton fields (It was back in Louisiana)
Let me hear it for the cotton fields
(Just about a mile from Texarkana)
You know that there's just no place like home

Well boy it sure feels good to breathe the air back home
You shoulda seen their faces when they seen how I grown
In them old cotton fields back home

WILDWOOD FLOWER

```
  C                           G7        C
I will twine and will mingle my waving black hair
                              G7    C
With the roses so red and the lilies so fair
                         F
The myrtle so green of an emerald hue
                         G7         C
The pale emanita and eyes look like blue
```

Oh he promised to love me, he promised love
To cherish me always all others above
I woke from my dream and my idol was clay
My passion for loving had vanished away

I'd dance and I'll sing and my life shall be gay
I'll charm every heart in the crowd I survey
Though my heart now is breaking he never shall know
How his name makes me tremble my pale cheeks to glow

Oh he taught me to love him, he called me his flower
A blossom to cheer him through life's weary hour
But now he has gone and left me alone
The wild flowers to weep and the wild birds to moan

I'll dance and I'll sing and my heart will be gay
I'll banish this weeping, drive troubles away
I'll live yet yo see him regret this dark hour
When he won and neglected the frail wildwood flower

YELLOW BIRD

```
C              G7           C
```
Yellow bird, up high in banana tree
```
C              G7           C
```
Yellow bird, you sit all alone like me
```
F              C
```
Did your lady friend, Leave your nest again

```
G7             C
```
That is very sad, Makes me feel so sad

```
F              C
```
You can fly away, In the sky away

```
G7                     C
```
You're more lucky than me

```
C              G7
```
I also had a pretty girl
```
               C
```
She's not with me today
```
                            G7
```
They're all the same the pretty girls
```
                            C
```
Take tenderness, then they fly away

Yellow bird, up high in banana tree
Yellow bird, you sit all alone like me
Let her fly away in the sky away
Pick a town and soon take from night to noon
Like that yellow moon, Like banana too
She might pick you some day

NEVER ON SUNDAY

```
  D                                  A          D
Oh, you can kiss me on a Monday, a Monday is very,
very good
                                   A
Or you can kiss me on a Tuesday, a Tuesday, Tuesday
                         D
In fact I wish you would
                                 A
Or you can kiss me on a Wednesday, a Thursday,
                        D
Friday and Saturday is best
                           A
But never, never on a Sunday, a Sunday, a Sunday
                           D
Cause that's my day of rest.
```

CHORUS
```
D         G            D
Most any day, you can be my guest
   A             D
Any day you say, but my day of rest
     G                    D
Just name the day that you lie the best
        A           D
Only stay away on my day of rest
```

Oh you can kiss me on a cool day, a hot day, a wet day,
 whichever one you choose
Or try to kiss me on a gray day, a May day,
a pay day ad see if I refuse
And if you make it on a bleak day, a freak day, a weekday,
 why you can be my guest
But never on a Sunday, a Sunday, a Sunday,
I one day I need a little rest

I DON'T HAVE A WOODEN HEART

C   F   C
Can't you see I love you, Please don't break my heart in two
                       F   G7   C
That's not hard to do, 'Cause I don't have a wooden heart
              F   C
And if you say goodbye, Then I know that I would cry
          C   F   G7   C
Maybe I would die, 'Cause I don't have a wooden heart

 C   G7   C
There's no strings upon this love of mine
 F   C
It was always you from the start
             F
Treat me nice ,Treat me good
    C
Treat me like you really should

'Cause I'm not made of wood
    F   G7   C
And I don't have a wooden heart

Muss i denn, muss i denn, Zum Stadtele hinaus
Stadtele hinaus, Und du, mein schat, bleibst hier?

There's no strings upon this love of mine
It was always you from the start
Sei mir gut, Sei mir gut
Sei mir wie du wirklich sollst
Wie du wirklich sollst
'Cause I don't have a wooden heart

ALL I HAVE TO DO IS DREAM
Everly Brothers

   C   Am   Dm7   G7
When I Want You   In My Arms
   C   Am   Dm   G7
when I want you   and all your charms
   C   Am
whenever i want you
F   G7   C   Am   F   G7
all li have to do is dream, dream, dream, dream.

   C   Am   Dm   G7
when li feel blue   in the night
   C   Am Dm   G7
and I need you   to hold me tight
   C   Am
 whenever I want you
F   G7   C   F   C   C7
all I have to do is dream.

F   Em
I can make you mine   taste your lips of wine
Dm   G7   C   C7
anytime night or day.
F   Em
only trouble is   gee whiz,
      D7   G7
I'm dreaming my life away.

   C   Am Dm   G7
I need you so   that li could die.
   C   Am Dm   G7
I love you so   and that is why.
      C   Am   F   G7   C F C
Whenever I want you all I have to is dream

THE SINGING NUN DOMINIQUE

CHORUS:
```
   G                      C
Dominique...nique..nique, over the
                 G          D
land he plods, and sings a little song.
     G                        C
Never asking for reward, he just talks about the Lord.
      G  D      G
He just talks about the Lord.
```

#1.
```
    C              G           D
G
At a time when Johnny Lackland, over England was the King.
      A                          A7        D
Dominique was in the backland, fighting sin  like anything.
```

EDELWEISS

```
G    D    G    C
```
Edelweiss, edelweiss
```
G    EM       C       D
```
Every morning you greet me
```
G         D     G       C
```
Small and white, clean and bright
```
 G        D       G
```
You look happy to meet me
```
D                         G
```
Blossom of snow may you bloom and grow
```
   C       A     D     D
```
Bloom and grow, forever
```
G    D    G    C
```
Edelweiss, edelweiss
```
  G         D           G    Am D
```
Bless my homeland forever

WHO'S SORRY NOW
by Louis Armstrong

RUN: G Gb F (all in F config) then to E7
E7
No gal made has got a shade on Sweet Georgia Brown,
A7
Two left feet, oh, so neat, Has Sweet Georgia Brown
D7
They all sigh, and want to die, For Sweet Georgia Brown!
D7   G   D7   G   RUN
I'll tell you just why, You know I don't lie, not much

E7
It's been said She knocks 'em dead, When she lands in town!
A7
Since she came, Why it's a shame, How she cools them down!
Em   B7   Em   B7
Fellows she can't get Are fellows she aint met

 G   Bb   F   E7
Georgia claimed her, Georgia named her,
A7   D7   G
Sweet Georgia Brown!

 C   E7
 Who's sorry now Who's sorry now
A7   D7
 Who's heart is aching for breaking each vow
G7   C
 Who's sad and blue who's crying too
D7   G7
 Just like I cried over you
C   E7

Right to the end just like a friend
```
A7                D7
```
I tried to warn you somehow
```
F          Fm  C          A7
```
You had your way now you must pay
```
D7         G7        C
```
I'm glad that you're sorry now
```
              E7
```
Right to the end just like a friend
```
A7                D7
```
I tried to warn you somehow
```
F             Fm  C        A7
```
You had your way now you must pay
```
D7         G7        C
```
I'm glad that you're sorry now

CECILIA- Simon and Garfunkel

CHORUS:
```
 G               C           G
Cecilia, you're breaking my heart
              C       G       D
You're shaking my confidence daily
    C    G       C          G
Oh Cec   ilia, I'm down on my knees
          C           G         D
I'm begging you please to come home
             G
Come on home
```
CHORUS
```
G                  C    G
Making love in the afternoon with Cecilia
 C   D       G
Up in my bedroom
                C      G
I got up to wash my face
                       C
When I come back to bed
            D        G
Someone's taken my place ...CHORUS


G                      C G C G D
Bo po bo bo ...
```

Jubilation, she loves me again
I fall on the floor and I laughing
Jubilation, she loves me again
I fall on the floor and I laughing
```
G                      C G C G C G D
Wo ho oooh ...
```

OB LA DI OB LA DAH
(Beatles)

```
C                             G7
```
Desmond had a barrow in the market place
```
F                    C
```
Molly is the singer in the band
```
C                         F
```
Desmond says to Molly girl I like your face
```
            C             G7            C
```
And Molly says this as she takes him by the hand
CHORUS
```
    C                    G7    F
```
Ob la di, ob la da, life goes on   on
```
C       G7      C
```
La la la la life goes on
```
    C                     G7    F
```
Ob lah di, ob la da, life goes on   on
```
C       G7      C
```
La la la la life goes on

Desmond takes a trolly to the jewlers store
Buys a twenty caral golden ring
Takes it back to Molly waiting at the door
Ans as he gives it to her she begins to sing
CHORUS

Happy ever after in the market place
Desmond lets the children lend a hand
Molly stays at home and does her pretty face
And in the evening still sings it with the band

NEVER ENDING SONG OF LOVE

G   D
I've got a never ending love for you
                           G
From now on that's all I want to do
                          D
From the first time we met I knew
           C   D   G
I'd have a never ending love for you
       C
After all this time of being alone
         G
To love one another live for

Live for each other
            C   D
From now on, from now on, from now on
         D
Yes its so good I can hardly stand
         G   D   G
This never ending love for you

KALINKA

CHORUS

```
Em   B7                           Em
Ka   lin   ka, ka lin ka, ka lin ka   ma ia
Ka   lin   ka  Ka lin Ka Ka lin ka of mine
         B7                          Em
V sa du ia  go  da ma lin ka, ma lin ka mo ia!
In the   ar  bor grows a ber ry as sweet as red wine
Em   B7                           Em
Ka   lin   ka, ka lin ka, ka lin ka   ma ia
Ka   lin   ka  Ka lin Ka Ka lin ka of mine
         B7                          Em         D
V sa du ia  go  da ma lin ka, ma lin ka mo ia!
In the   ar  bor grows a ber ry as sweet as red wine


         G      D7   G                D7    G
Akh, pod  sos   no   iv,      pod ze le   no iv,
 under  the oak  tree, under the shade tree
C              A7      D  Em7    D
Spat' po lo zhi te  vy  me      nia!
I'll   lie    down and fall a   aleep
     G     D7   G          D7    G
A  ai    liu   li  liu  li Ai liu  li
Ah Oh   liu   li   liu  li Ai Liu Li
C              Am     D7  Am6   B7
Spat' po lo zhi te  vy  me    nya    Ka
I'll   lie    down and fall a    sleep   Ka...
```

GUANTANAMERA

Intro: D Em A A (x2)

        D   Em   A
Yo soy un hombre sincero,
         D   Em   A
de donde crece la palma
        D   Em A   G   A
Yo soy un hombre sincero,
     G   A
de donde crece la palma
       D   Em A   D   Em A
Y antes de morirme quiero echar
   D   Em   A
mis versos de alma

CHORUS:
G   A   D   A
Guantanamera, guajira guantanamera
D   Em A   D   Em A
Guantanamera, guajira guantanamera

.

I'LL SEE YOU IN MY DREAMS
by Gus Kahn and Isham Jones

Intro: [F] [F6] [FM7] [F6] (4 times)
[F] [F6] [FM7] [F6]   D7   D   D9   D
Tho' the days are long Twilight sings a song
 [G7]   [Bbm6]   [C]   [F][F6][FM7][F6]
Of the happi-ness   that used to be.
[Am]   [E7]   E7   Am
Soon my eyes will close. Soon I'll find repose
 [C]   [C#dim]   [Dm]   [G7]   [C][CM7][C7]
And in dreams you're always near to me ………..

[Bb]   [Bb6] [BbM7] [Bbm6] [F6]   [E7] [E7-2] [F6]
I'll see you in   my   dreams. Hold you in my   dreams
 [D7]   [D7sus2]   [D7]   [G7]   [C] [CM7]
[C7]
Someone took you out of my arms. Still I feel the thrill of your charms

 [Bb]   [Bb6] [BbM7] [Bbm6]   [F]   [E7] [E7-2] [F6]
Lips that once were mine.   Tender eyes that shine
[Cm6]   [D7] [D7] [A7]   [Dm] [F7]
They will light my   way tonight
[Bb]   [Bbm6] [C] [F]
I'll see you in   my dreams

MARTY ROBBINS

EL PASO (Marty Robbins)

C   Dm   G7
Out in the West Texas town of El Paso,
G7   C
I fell in love with a Mexican girl.
                           Dm
Nighttime would find me in Rosa's cantina,
G7   C
Music would play and Felina would whirl.
C   Dm
Blacker than night were the eyes of Felina,
 G7   C
wicked and evil while casting a spell.
C   Dm
My love was deep for this Mexican maiden,
 G7   C
I was in love but in vain I could tell.
    F   Bb   F
One night a wild young cowboy came in,
       Bb   C7   C7
wild as the West Texas wind. Flashing
Dashing and daring, a drink he was sharing
                         F
with wicked Felina, the girl that I loved
. G7   C   Dm
So in anger, I challenged his right for the love of this maiden,
G7   C
down went his hand for the gun that he wore.
C   Dm
My challenge was answered in less than a heart beat,
G7   C
the handsome young stranger lay dead on the floor.
C   Dm
My challenge was answered in less than a heart beat,
G7   C
the handsome young stranger lay dead on the floor

BIG IRON
Marty Robbins

Am   Em   Am
(8) counts...(2) counts (1) count
```
      C                                  Am
To the town of Agua Fria rode a stranger one fine day
      C                                              Am
Hardly s poke to folks around him didn't have too much to say
      F                         C
No one  dared to ask his business no one dared to make a slip
                                              Am
For the stranger there among them had a  big iron on his hip
F             C
Big iron on his hip
```

It was early in the morning when he rode into the town
He came riding from the south side slowly lookin' all around
He's an outlaw loose and running came the whisper from each lip
And he's here to do some business with the big iron on his hip
Big iron on his hip

In this town there lived an outlaw by thename of Texas Red
Many men had tried to take him and that many men were dead
He was vicious and a killer though a youth of twenty four
And the notches on his pistol numbered one an nineteen more
One and nineteen more

Now the stranger started talking made it plain to folks around
Was an Arizona ranger wouldn't be too long in town
He came here to take an outlaw back alive or maybe dead
And he said it didn't matter he was after Texas Red
After TexasRed

RUNNING GUN
Marty Robbins

[D] I rode out of Kansas City, going south to Mexi[G7]co
[A] I was running dodging danger, left the girl that I [G7] loved [D] so
Far behind lay Kansas City and the [G7] past that I had earned
[A] Twenty notches on my six gun marked the [G7] lessons I had [D] learned
[G7] Many times I sold my fast gun for a [D] place to lay my head
[G7] Till the nights began to haunt me by the [D] men that I lay [A] dead
[D] Couldn't stand it any longer with the [G7] life that I'd begun
[A] So I said good-bye to Jeannie and [G7] became a running [D] gun

I rode into Amarillo as the sun sank in the west
My thoughts in Kansas City and the girl that I love best
As I smiled and kissed her gently and then turned around to go
Said I'd send for her to meet me when I reached old Mexico
I had barely left the saddle and my foot just touched the ground
When a cold voice from the shadows told me not to turn around
Said he knew about my fast gun, new the price paid by the law
Challenged by a bounty hunter, so I turned around to draw

THE HANGIN' TREE
Marty Robbins

```
C                    Am
 I came to town to search for gold
       C              G
And I brought with me a memory
         Am           C
And seem to hear the night wind cry
     Am             C
Go hang your dreams on the hangin tree
     Am                   C
Your (dreams of love that could never be
                    G       C
Hang your faded (dreams on the hangin tree
```

I searched for gold and I found my gold
And I found a girl who loved just me
And I wish that I could love her too
But I left my heart on the hangin tree
I left my heart with a memory
And a faded dream on the hangin tree

```
        F              G
That's when I knew that the hangin tree
       F            C
Was a tree of life, new life for me
  F          C
A tree of hope new hope for me
  F            C
A tree of love new (love for me
                  F
The hangin tree, the hangin tree,
  C
 the hangin tree
```

DEVIL WOMAN
Marty Robbins

```
E                          B
```
I told Mary about it, I Told her about a great sin

Mary cried and forgave me
```
              E
```
Then Mary took me back again

Said if I wanted my freedom
```
              A
```
I could be free ever more
```
              E
```
But I don't want to be, and I don't want to see
```
B      E
```
Mary cry anymore
```
          B
```
Chorus
```
B
```
 Oh DEVIL WOMAN
```
        E
```
 DEVIL WOMAN let go of me
```
       B
```
DEVIL WOMAN let me be, and leave me alone
```
   E
```
I want to go home

Mary is waiting and weeping, Down in our shack by the sea
Even after I hurt her, Mary's still in love with me
DEVIL WOMAN it's over, Trapped no more by your charm
Cause I don't want to stay, I want to get away
Woman let go of my arm

JOHN DENVER

COUNTRY ROADS
(John Denver)

```
 C              Am
Almost  heaven West Virginia
G              F          C
Blue Ridge Mountains, Shenandoah River
               Am
Life is old there, older than the trees,
G                       F              C
Younger than the mountains, growin like a breeze
```
CHORUS
```
C                    G          Am         F
```
Country roads, take me home, to the place I belong
```
         C            G        F           C
```
West Virginia, mountain momma, take me home, country roads
```
Am       G         C                  Am
I hear her voice in the morning hour she calls me,
    F      C        G
The radio reminds of my home far away
    Am          G Bb      F
And driven' down the road I get a feelin that
    C                 G7           F
I should have been home yesterday, yesterday,
```
CHORUS

```
C              Am
All my mem'ries gather round her,
G      F       C
Miners lady stranger to blue water
              Am
Dark and dusty painted on the sky
G                  F              C
Misty taste of moonshine, tear drops in my eye
```
CHORUS

ANNIES SONG
John Denver

`G            C D   Em    C          G`
You fill up my senses, like a night in the forest.
`G            C D     Am    C        D`
Like a mountain in springtime, like a walk in the rain.
`G            C D       Em    C      G`
Like a storm in the desert, like a sleepy blue ocean.
`G            C D   Am  D    G`
You fill up my senses, come fill me again.
`G            C D   Em    C          G`
Come let me love you, let me give my life for you.
`G              C  D    Am    C      D`
Let me drown in your laughter, let me die in your arms.
`G            C  D   Em    C       G`
Let me lay down beside you, let me always be with you.
`G           C D    Am    D    G`
Come let me love you, come love me again.
HUM FIRST FIVE LINES

`Em     C          G`
Let me give my life to you
`G       C  D    Am    D    G`
Come let me love you, Come love me again

`G            C D   Em    C       G`
You fill up my senses, like a night in the forest.
`G             C   D    Am   C       D`
Like a mountain in spring time, like a walk in the rain.
`G            C D    Em    C       G`
Like a storm in the desert, like a sleepy blue ocean.
`G            C D    Am  D    G`
You fill up my senses, come fill me again.

FOR BABY (FOR BOBBIE)}
John Denver

```
    G        C          G
I'll walk in the rain by your side,
  C        D          G
I'll cling to the warmth of your tiny hand,
  C    D          G   Em
I'll do anything to help you understand,
  G           D       G
I love you more than anybody can.


       C      D       G
And the wind will whisper your name to me;
C          D        G
Little birds will sing along in time;
  C            D       G     C
The leaves will bow down when you walk by,
   G     D      G
And morning bells will chime.
```

I'll be there when you're feeling down
To kiss away the tears if you cry.
I'll share with you all the happiness I've found,
A reflection of the love in your eyes.

And I'll sing you the songs of the rainbow,
 Whisper of the joy that is mine;
The leaves will bow down when you walk by,
And morning bells will chime.

GOOD TO BE BACK HOME AGAIN (John Denver)

G   C
There's a storm across the valley and clouds are rolling in
　　　D7   G
The afternoon is heavy on my shoulder
　　　　　　　　　　　　　　　C
There's a truck out on the four lane a mile or more away
　　　D7   G
The whining of his wheels just makes it colder
G   C
He's an hour away from ridden on your prayers up in the sky
　　G7   G
And Ten days on the road are nearly gone
　　　　　G   C
There's a fire softly burning, suppers on the stove
　　　D7   G   D7
It's the light in your eyes that makes him warm
C   D   DC   D7
Hey, it's good to be back home again,
C   D   G   C
sometimes this old farm feels like a long lost friend
　　　D7   G
Yes hey it's good to be back home again

There's all the news to tell him, how'd you spend your time
What's the latest thing the neighbours say
And your mother called last Friday, sunshine made her cry
You felt the baby move just yesterday

Oh the time that I can lay this tired old body down
Feel your fingers feather soft upon me
The kisses that

GREEN GREEN GRASS OF HOME
(John Denver)

G   C   G
The old town looks the same as I step down from the train
                                      D7
And there to meet me is my mama and papa
                G   G7
Down the road I look and there runs Mary
C
Pair of golden lips like cherries
  G   D7   G
It's good to touch the green, green grass of home
 G
Yes they'll all come to meet me
C
Arms reaching, smiling sweetly
  G   D7   G
It's good to touch the green green grass of home

The old house is still standing though the paint is cracked and dry
And there's the old oak tree that I used to play on
Down the lane I walk with my sweetheart Mary
Pair of golden lips like cherry
It's good to touch the green, green grass of home

Then I awake and around me are four grey walls that surround me
And I realize I/m only dreaming
For theres a God and a sad padre
Arm in arm we'll walk at day break
Again I'll touch the green, green grass of home

Yes they'll all come to meet me
Arms reaching, smiling sweetly
It's good to touch the green green grass of home

CALYPSO
(John Denver)

G
To sail on a dream on a crystal clear ocean
                                  D
To ride on the crest of the wild raging storm
     G
To work in the service of life and the living
                                 D
In search of the answers to questions unknown

C   G
Aye Calypso the places you've been to
     C   G   DC
The things that you've shown us, the stories you tell
C   G
Aye   Calypso I sing to your spirit
   C   /G   D   G
The men who have served you so long and so well

     D   C   G   D C
Hi dee ay ee ooo   ee ee oh ee
C   G   D   C
Oh del ooh do   do do ooh
G   C   G   D
Oh del oh yay eeee ee
C   G   D G   C G C
Do del aye ee ay yee ee

THANK GOD I'M A COUNTRY BOY
(John Denver)

```
      G                         C
Well, life on the farm is kind a laid back
      G                       F        D7
Ain't much an old country boy like me can hack
    G                      C
It's early to rise, early in the sack
    G         D7      G
Thank God I'm a country boy
```

A simple kinda a life never did me no harm
Raisen' me a family and workin' on a farm
My days are still filled with an easy country charm
Thank God I'm a country boy

CHORUS
```
        G                   D7
Well I  got me a fine wife, I got me old fiddle.
            G                   E7
When the sun's comin' up I got cakes on the griddle;
            G                       C
and life ain't nothin' but a funny, funny riddle:
        G         D7     G
Thank God I'm a country boy.
```

GRAMMAS FEATHER BED

D   G   D   A
When I was a little bitty boy , just up off the floor
D   G
We used to go down to Grandma's house
D   A   D
Every month end or so
          D   G
We'd have chicken pie, country ham
D   A
Home-made butter on the bread
        D   G
But the best darn thing about Grandma'a house
      A   D
Was the great big feather bed
CHORUS
     D
It was nine feet high and six feet wide
G   D
Soft as a downy chick
    D
It was made of the feathers of four-eleven geese
    E7   A
And a while roll of clothe for the tick
    D
It could hold eight kids and four hound dogs
    G   D
And the piggy that we stole form the shed
  D   G
Didn't get much sleep but we had alot of fun
A   D
In Grandma's feather bed

THE NIGHT THEY DROVE OLD DIXIE
(J Denver)

```
C      Am            C         Am
```
Virgil Caine is the name, I served on the Dansyl Train
```
C       Am           C         Am
```
So much cavalry came and tore up the tracks again
```
C            Am            C          Am
```
In the summer of sixty-five we were hungry just barely alive
```
C            Am                     Am      D
```
By May the tenth Richmond had fell it's a time I remember so well

CHORUS
```
   C         Am         C        Am
```
The night they drove old Dixie down and the bells were ringin'
```
   C         Am         C        Am
```
The night they drove old Dixie down and the people were singin
```
       C         Am        D      F      Am
```
They went la na na na na la na na na na na na na

Back home in Tennessee my wife called out for me
Say Virgil come quick and see there goes Robert E Lee
I don't mind choppin' wood and I don't care if da money ain't good
You take what you need and save the rest but they should never have taken the very best
CHORUS
Like my father before me he was a workin' man
Like my brother above me he took a rebel's stand
He was just eighteen proud and brave when a Yankee laid him in his grave
I swear by the blood beneath my feet
You can't raise a Caine back up when he's in defeat

ABBA

I HAVE A DREAM (Abba)

INTRO DD CC GG

```
 G          C                    G
```
I have a dream, a song to sing
```
            C              G
```
To help me cope with anything
```
              D         G
```
If you see the wonder of a fairy tale
```
              D              G
```
You can take the future even if you fail

CHORUS:
```
G           C                       D      G
```
I believe in angels, something good in everything I see
```
 G          C                    D      G
```
I believe in angels, when I know the time is right for me
```
G           C              G
```
I'll cross the stream, I have a dream

I have a dream, a fantasy
To help me through reality
And my destination makes it worth the while
Pushing through the darkness, still another mile

CHORUS:

I have a dream, a song to sing
To help me cope with anything
If you see the wonder, of a fairy tale
You can take the future, even if you fail

REPEAT CHORUS

TAKE A CHANCE ON ME (Abba)

Chorus:

                  G
If you change your mind, I'm the first in line

                           D
Honey I'm still free, take a chance on me

If you need me let me know, gonna be around

                         G
If you got no place to go when you're feelin' down

      G
If you're all alone, when the pretty birds have flown

                         D
Honey I'm still free, take a chance on me

Gonna do my very best, and it ain't no lie

                     G
If you put me to the test, if you let me try
 D
Take a chance on me   (that's all I ask of you, honey) - 1st time

                   (c'mon, give me a break, man)   - 2nd time
     D
Take a chance on me
Am#   Am# 003321
We can go dancing, we can go walking
  G
As long as we're together
Am
Listen to some music, maybe just slow and
G
Get to know me better

                       F
Cause you know I've got, so much that I wanna do
C   F

When I dream I'm alone with you, it's magic
F   C
You want to leave it there, afraid of a love affair
                 D
But I think you know, that I can't let go

(Chorus)
          Am
Oh you can take your chance baby, I'm in no hurry
G
Ooh I'm gonna get you
Am
You're the one that hurt me, baby don't worry
G
I ain't gonna let you
F
My love is strong enough
C   F
To last when things are rough, it's magic
F   CE
You say that I waste my time, but I can't get you off my mind
D
Oh I can't let go, cause I love you so

(Chorus)
Here replace the first line with: "Pa pa pa pa pam pa pa pa pa pam."

EAGLE (Abba)

Intro chords: Em   Am

Em
They came flyin' from far away, now I'm under their spell
                            D   Em
I love hearing the stories that they tell
They've seen places beyond my land and they've found
       Bm
new horizons
Em   D   Em
They speak strangely but I understand
                    B7 Em
And I dream I'm an eagle
                          A7
And I dream I can spread my wings

(CHORUS)
     G   D   Em   D
Flyin' high, high, I'm a bird in the sky
     Em   D   Em
I'm an eagle that rides on the breeze
High, high, what a feeling to fly
Over mountains and forests and seas
And to go anywhere that I please

As all good friends we talk all night, and we fly wing to wing
I have questions and they know everything
There's no limit to what I feel, we climb higher and higher
Am I dreamin' or is it all real

Is it true I'm an eagle
Is it true I can spread my wings

THE PIPER (Abba)

Bm   (Bm 014432)
They came from the hills
And they came from the valleys and the plains
They struggled in the cold
In the heat and the snow and in the rain
     A   Bm
Came to hear him play
Bm   A   Bm   D   E
Play their minds away)

CHORUS:
A   D   A
We're all following a strange melody
                   D   E
We're all summoned by a tune
 F#m   Bm   F#m   (F#m 244222)
We're following the piper
      D   E   A   E
And we dance beneath the moon)
A D A D E
We're following the piper
And we dance beneath the moon for him
And we dance beneath the moon
A E/G#bass   C#m F#m   F#m E   C#m G# C#m
Sub luna saltamus
VERSE
CHORUS
VERSE
CHORUS
Play their minds away

BOB DYLAN

BLOWIN' IN THE WIND
(Bob Dylan)

```
C          F          C
How many roads must a man walk down
           F      C      G7
Before you call him a man
         C        F           C
Yes and how many seas must a white dove sail
              F        G        G7
Before she sleeps in the sand
         C        F           C
Yes' n how many times must the cannon ball fly
              F     C
before they're forever banned
```
CHORUS
```
   F         G7        C          Am
The answer my friend is blowin in the wind
   F         G7        C
The answer is blowin in the wind
```

How many times must a man look up
Before he can see the sky
Yes and how many ears must one man have
Before he can ear people cry?
Yes an how many deaths will it take till he knows
That too many people have died?
CHORUS The answer my friend....

How many years can a mountain exist
Before it is washed to the sea?
Yes, 'n how many years can some people exist
Before they're allowed to be free?
Yes, 'n how many times can a man turn his head
Pretending he just doesn't see?

DON'T THINK TWICE, ITS ALL RIGHT
(Bob Dylan)

```
 G              D            Em
It ain't no use to sit and wonder why babe
C                 D7
It don't matter any how
 G              D            Em
Aint no use to sit and wonder why babe
C                 D7
If you don't know by now
           G                G7
When the rooster crows at the break of dawn
C                 A7
Look out your window and I'll be gone
G              Em      C
Youre the reason I'm travellin on
G       D7         G
Don't think twice, its all right
```

It ain't no use in turn' on your light babe
That light I never knowed
It ain't no use in turnin' on your light babe
I'm on the dark side of the road
Still I wish there was somethin' you would do or say
To try and make me change my mind and stay
We never did too much talikn' anyway
So don't think twice, it's all right

I'm walking down that lonesome road babe
Where I'm bound I can't tell
But goodbyes too good a word Gal
So I'll just say fare thee well
I ain't sayin' you treated me unkind
You could have done better but I don't mind
You just wasted my precious time
But don't think twice, it's all right

MR TAMBOURINE MAN
(Bob Dylan)

```
     G         A            D              G
Hey Mr Tambourine man play a song for me
        D          G       Em       A
I'm not sleepy and there is no place I'm goin to
  G       A          D              G
Hey, Mr Tambourine man play a song for me
        D       G      Em       A        D    G  D
In the jingle jangle morin I'll come following you


           G            A          D             G
Though I know that evenins empire  has returned into sand
D             G           D           G       Em   A
Vanished from my hand Left me blindly here to stand but still not
sleepin
   G         A          D           G  D           G
My weariness amazes me I'm branded on my feet, I have no one to
meet
           D          G         Em      A
And the ancient empty streets too dead for dreamin'
```

RERAIN

Take me on a trip upon your magic swirlin' ship
My senses have been stripped, my hands can't feel the grip
My toes too numb to step, wait only for my boot heels
To be wanderin'
I'm ready to go anywhere, I'm ready for to fade
Into my own parade, cast you dancin' spell my way
I promise to go under it

REFRAIN

Though you might hear laugh'n spinnin' swingin' madley across
the sun
It's not aimed at anyone, it's just escapin' on the run
And but for the sky there are no fences facin'
And if you vague traces of skippin' reels of rhyme

TIMES THEY ARE A CHANGIN'
(Bob Dylan)

```
  G              Em         C         G
Come gather round people wherever you roam
  G              Am    C              D
And admit that the waters around you have grown
  G          Em          C              G
And accept that soon you'll be drenched to the bone
            Am         D
If your time to you is worth savin'
                       D7          Gmaj7     D
Then you better start swimming or you'll sing like a stone
     G            C  D    G
For the times they are a chang    in'
```

INTERLUDE FOR VERSES 3,4
G   Em D   D7   Gmaj7   D

Come writers and critics who prophecies your pen
And keep your eyes wide. The chances won't come again
And don't speak too soon For the wheel's in still in spin
And there's no tellin' who That it's naming
For the loser now Will be later to win
For the times the ara a changin'

Come mothers and fathers, throughout the land
And don't criticize what you can't understand
Your sons and your daughters are beyond your command
Your old road is rapidly agin'
Please get out the new one if you can't lend your hand
For the times they are a changin'

Come senators, congressmaen, pease heed the call
Don't stand in the doorway, don't block the hall
For he that get's hurt will be he who has staled
There's a battle outside and it's ragin'
It'll soon shake your windows and rattle your wall
For the times they are a changin'

IT AIN'T ME BABE
(Bob Dylan)

```
G            C        G          D          G   C G
Go away from my window, leave at your own chosen speed
G                   C        G    D      G   C G
I'm not the one you want babe, I'm not the one you need
  Bm              Am           Bm             Am
You say you're worken' for some never weak but always strong
  Bm           Am             Bm            Am
To protect you and defend you whether you are right or wrong
  C               D
Someone to open every door
```
CHORUS

```
        G    C    D       G
But it ain't me babe, no, no, no it ain't me babe
    C     D    G
It ain't me you're lookin' for, Babe
G  C   G   D7  G   C  G
```

Go lightly from the ledge Babe, go lightly on the ground
I'm not the one you want Babe, I will only let you down
You say you're lookin' for some on Who will promise never to part
Someone to close his eyes for you, someone to close your heart
Someone who will die for you an' more
CHORUS

Go melt back into the night Babe,
everything inside is made of stone
There's nothing in here moving, n' anyway I'm not alone
You say you're lookin' for someone
Who'll pick you up each time you fall
To gathe flowers constantly, an' come each time you call
A lover for your life an' nothing more
CHORUS

A HARD RAINS GONNA FALL
(Bob Dylan)

INTRO C Fmaj7 C

```
     C              Fmaj7        C
Oh, where have you been, my blue-eyed son?
     C                              G
Oh, where have you been, my darling young one?
     F                G(3)          C
I've stumbled on the side of twelve misty mountains,
     F                G(3)          C
I've walked and I've crawled on six crooked highways,
     F                G(3)          C
I've stepped in the middle of seven sad forests,
     F                G(3)          C
I've been out in front of a dozen dead oceans,
     F                G(3)          C
I've been ten thousand miles in the mouth of a graveyard,
           C       G       C       F
And it's a hard, and it's a hard, it's a hard, and it's a hard,
           C    G     C    Fmay7   C
And it's a hard rain's a-gonna fall.
```

Oh, what did you see, my blue-eyed son?
Oh, what did you see, my darling young one?
I saw a newborn baby with wild wolves all around it,
I saw a highway of diamonds with nobody on it,
I saw a black branch with blood that kept drippin',
I saw a room full of men with their hammers a-bleedin',
I saw a white ladder all covered with water,
I saw ten thousand talkers whose tongues were all broken,

GOTTA TRAVEL ON
(Bob Dylan)

```
      G
Done laid around, done stayed around This old town too long
                            C           G
Summer's almost gone, winter's coming on

Done laid around, done stayed around This old town too long
        Am7         D7          G
And it seems like I've got to travel on
        Am7         D7          G
And it seems like I've got to travel on.
```

Papa writes to Johnny, "Johnny, can't you come home ?
Johnny, can't you come home ? Johnny, can't you come home ?"
Papa writes to Johnny, "Johnny, can't you come home ?"
Johnny's been out on the road too long
Done laid around, done stayed around This old town too long
And it seems like I've got to travel on
And it seems like I've got to travel on.

That silly wind will soon begin and I'll be on my way
Going home to stay, going home to stay
That silly wind will soon begin and I'll be on my way
And I feel like I just want to travel on
Done laid around, done stayed around This old town too long
And it seems like I've got to travel on
And it seems like I've got to travel on.

There's a lonesome freight at 6.08 coming through the town
I'll be homeward bound, I'll be homeward bound
There's a lonesome freight at 6.08 coming through the town
And I feel like I just want to travel on
Done laid around, done stayed around This old town too long
And it seems like I've got to travel on
And it seems like I've got to travel on.

Am7 002213

ROGER WHITTAKER

58. LOVE IS BLUE

```
Am   D   Am   D
Am   D              G    Am      C
Blue blue, my world is blue, blue is my world
     G          Am
Now I'm without you
Am    D         G    Am      C
Grey, grey my life is grey, Cold is my heart
     E         Am
since you went away
C    F C            F       C
When we met how the bright sun shone
Dm      F           G7
Then love died now the rainbow is gone
Am    D       G        G
Black, black the nights I've known
Am        C     D       Am
Longing for you so lost and alone
```

Gone gone the love we knew
Blue is my world now I'm without you
Red, red, my eyes are red
Crying for you alone in my bed
Green green, my jealous heart
I doubted you and now were apart

When we met how the bright sun shone
Then love died now the rainbow is gone
Black, black the nights I've known
Longing for you so lost and alone
Blue blue, my world is blue
Blue is my world, I'm without you

DURHAM TOWN
(Roger Whittacker)

CHORUS

| F | C | Bb | C7 |

I've got ta leave old Durham town

| F | Bb | C | F |

I've got ta leave old Durham town

| | A | Dm | Gm |

I've got ta leave old Durham town

| | F/C | C7 | F |

And that leavin's gonna get me down

| F | C | Bb | C7 |

Back in nineteen fourty four,

| Dm | A7/E | Dm/F | A7 |

I remember daddy walkin out the door

| F | C7 | Bb | C7 |

Momma told me he was goin' to war

| | Dm | A7 | |

He was leavin', leavin, leavin', leavin' me Now
CHORUS

I was a boy I spent my time
Sittin' on the banks of the river Tyne
Watchin' all the ships goin' down the line
They we leavin', leavin', leavin', leavin' me Now
CHORUS

Last week moma passed away
Goodbye son is all she'd say
There's no call for me to stay
So I'm leavin', leavin, leavin', leavin' free Now
CHORUS

NEW WORLD IN THE MORNING
Roger Whittaker

Chorus
```
 C      Em7      Am         Am7     (Am7 002213)
```
Everybody talks about a new world in the morning,
```
F            C    G7
```
new world in the morning, so they sa-a-a-ay well
```
C       Em7      Am         Am7
```
I myself don't talk about a new world in the morning
```
F                 Am
```
New world in the morning that's today.

```
       F     G7    C
```
And I can feel a new tomorrow coming on, and I
```
F       G7    C   G7
```
don't know why I have to make a so-o-o-ng. Well
```
C     Em7     Am         Am7
```
everybody talks about a new world in the morning,
```
F               Am
```
new world in the morning takes too long.

(Chorus)
I met a man who had a dream he had since he was twenty
I met that man when he was eighty-o-o-o-o-ne.
 He said, Too many folks just stand and wait until the morning.
 Don't they know tomorrow never comes.

THE LAST FARWELL
Roger Whittaker

Verse#1:

    C   G   C
There's a ship lies rigged and ready in the harbor
C   C7   F
tomorrow for ol' England she sails
    Dm   F   Dm   F
far away from your land of endless sunshine
    Dm   F   G
to my land full of rainy skies and gales
   C   G   C   G
and I shall be on board that ship tomorrow
C   C7   F
though my heart is full of tears at this farewell

Chorus:

Dm G   C   Am   Dm   G7
For you are beautiful and I have loved you dearly
     Dm   G7   C
more dearly than the spoken word can tell
Dm G   C   Am   Dm   G7
for you are beautiful and I have loved you dearly
   Dm   G7   C
more dearly than the spoken word can tell

Verse#2

I heard there's a wicked war a blazing
and the taste of war I know so very well
Even now I see that foreign flag a raising
their guns on fire as we sailed into hell
I have no fear of death it brings no sorrow
but how bitter will be this last farewell

Chorus:

RIVER LADY

G
The day the river freezes
    Am
Is the day it won't seem fair
       C
'Cause they'll come to get the River Lady
  C   G
And I don't think they'll care

G
I know they'll scrape her paint off
    Am
In their same old foolish ways
    C
Now the people see the river
  C   G
But the old ships gone away

CHORUS
G   C
Water turns cold and gets ta freezin'
             G
Before you even know it, the old girl's easin'
      Bm
Away from her berth, round by the point
    C
And out of our view
  C
Off in the mist, her engine's poundin'
  G
Like on the banks, that old horn's soundin'
  Bm   C
A little goodbye, a little I'll do what I must do
  Bm   D   G
A little goodbye, a little I'll do what I must do

IRISH MELODIES

COCKLES AND MUSSELS

```
C            Am       Dm            G7
```
In Dublins fair city where girls are so pretty
```
   C       A7        D7      G7
```
I first set my eyes on sweet Molly Malone
```
            C                Am           Dm           G7
```
As she wheeled her wheelbarrow through streets broad and narrow
```
            C   F   C    F C    G7  C
```
Crying cockles and mussels a live a live oh

CHORUS
```
 C       Am  Dm    G7
```
A live a live oh alive alive oh
```
        C    F   C    F C   G7   C
```
Crying cockles and mussels A live a live oh

She was a fish monger but sure twas a wonder
For so went her father and mother before
As they each pushed their wheel barrow
through streets broad and narrow
Crying Cockles and mussels, alive, alive oh

CHORUS

DANNY BOY
Frederick Edward Weatherby

    C   G7   F
Oh Danny Boy the pipes are calling
   Fm   C   Am6   Fm6   G7
From glen to glen and down the mountain side   (Fm 002111)
           C   C7   (Am6 002212)
The summers gone and all the roses falling   (Fm6 000111)
  Fm C/G   G7   C (Em6 022020)
It's you It's you must go and I must bide   (Am7 002213)

                           (C9 032330)
No Chord   C   F6   G7   Am7 (F6 000211)
But come ye back when sum-mers in the meadow
      Am   F6   Em6   D7   G7
Or when the valleys hushed and white with snow
    C C9 F F3dim C E7 Am
Tis' I'll be there in sunshine or in shadow
Fm6   C/G   Am7 F6   G7   C
Oh Danny Boy Oh Danny Boy I love you so

But if you come and all the flowers are dieing
and I am dead as dead I well may be
You'll come and find the place where I am lieing
And kneel and say an ave there for me

STAR OF THE COUNTY DOWN

   Em   G   D
Near to Banbridge Town, in the County Down
  Em   D
One morning in July,
   Em   G   D
Down a boreen green came a sweet colleen,
    Em   Am   Em
And she smiled as she passed me by;
 G   D
Oh, she looked so neat from her two white feet
   Em   Am   D
To the sheen of her nut-brown hair,
   Em   G   D
Sure the coaxing elf, I'd to shake myself
 Em   Am   Em
To make sure I was standing there

      G   D
Oh, from Bantry Bay up to Derry Quay,
   Em   D
And from Galway to Dublin town,
 Em   G   D
No maid I've seen like the brown colleen
  Em   Am   Em
That I met in the County Down.

WHISKEY IN THE JAR

C   Am
As I was going over the Kilmagenny mountain
 F   Am   C   Am
I met with captain Farrell and his money he was counting.
C   Am
I first produced my pistol, and produced my rapier.
 F   C   Am
Said stand and deliver, for I am a bold deceiver,
CHORUS
      G7   C
musha ring dumma do damma da

whack for the daddy 'ol
F
whack for the daddy 'ol
 G7   C
there's whiskey in the jar

I counted out his money, and it made a pretty penny.
I put it in my pocket and I brought it home to Jenny.
She said and she swore, that she never would deceive me,
but the devil take the women, for they never can be easy
CHORUS
I went into my chamber, for to take a slumber,
I dreamt of gold and jewels and for sure it was no wonder.
But Jenny took my charges and she filled them up with water,
and sent for captain Farrel to be ready for the slaughter.
CHORUS
It was early in the morning, before I rose to travel,
the guards were all around me and likewise captain Farrel.
I first produced my pistol, for she stole away my rapier,
but I couldn't shoot the water so a prisoner I was taken.

THERE IS A TAVERN IN THIS TOWN

     C
There is a tavern in the town, in the town
                                    G7
And there my true love sits him down, sits him down
    C   F
And drinks his wine mid laughter free
  G7   C
And never never thinks of me
  G7
Fare the well for I must leave thee
      C
Do not let the parting grieve thee
        G   C   F   C
And remember that the best of friends must part, must part
C
Adieu, adieu, kind friends adieu
                    G7
I can no longer stay with you, stay with you
  C   F
I'll hang my harp on a weeping willow tree
 G7   C   G7 C
And may the world go well with thee

THE WILD COLONIAL BOY

C   F   G7   C
There was a wild colonial boy, Jack Duggin was his name
                        G   G7   C
He was born and raised in Ireland, in a place called Castlemain
               G   G7   C
He was his fathers only son, his mothers pride and joy,
  G7 F   G   G6 G7 C
And dearly did his parents love, the wild colonial boy.

At the early age of 16 years, Jack left his native home,
And to Austrailia's sunny shores, he was inclined to roam,
He roobed the Lordly squatters, their flocks he would destroy,
A terror to Austrailia was, the wild colonial boy.

One morning on the prairie, as Jack he rode along,
While listening to the mocking birds, singing a cheerful song,
Up jumped three troopers fierce and grim, Kelly, Davis, and Fitzroy,
They all set out to capture him, The wild colonial boy.

Surrender now Jack Duggin, for you see we're three to one,
Surrender in the Queens own name, for you are a plundering son,
Jack drew two pistols from his belt, and fired upon Fitzroy
I'll fight but not surrender cried the wild colonial boy.

He fired point blank and Kelly and brought him to the ground,
He fired a shot at Davis too, who fell dead upon the sound,

THE UNICORN SONG
Irish Rovers   Shel Silverstein

```
   C                        Dm
A long time ago when the earth was green
         G                          C
There was more kinds of animals than you'd ever seen
   C                        Dm
They'd run around free while the world was being born
         C                    Dm   G   C
But the loveliest of them all was the u--ni--corn
```

Chorus:
```
            C                   Dm
There was green alligators   and long necked geese
     G                        C
Some humpy back camels  and some chimpanzees
   C                         Dm
Cats and rats and elephants but sure as you're born
       C                 Dm  G   C
The loveliest of all was the u  --ni--corn
```

   But the Lord seen some sinnin' and it caused him pain
   He said "Stand back - I'm gonna make it rain
   So hey brother Noah, I'll tell you what to do,
   Build me a floating zoo."

Chorus:
   And you take two alligators and a couple of geese
   Two hump back camels and two chimpanzees
   Two cats, two rats, two elephants but sure as you're born
   Noah, don't you forget my u--ni--corn.

BONEY M

RASPUTIN
(Boney M)

      Am
There lived a certain man in Russia long ago,
      Dm   E   Am he was
big and strong, in his eyes a flaming glow,

Most people looked at him with terror and with fear,
      Dm   E   Am
but to Moscow chicks he was such a lovely dear.

                                          Dm   E
He could preach the Bible like a preacher, full of
     E
ecstasy and fire.
  Am   Dm   E
But he also was the kind of teacher, women would
Am
desire.

CHORUS
Am   C   D   A
Ra-Ra-Rasputin, lover of the Russian queen,
G   D   A
Here was a cat that really was done.
      C   D   A
Ra-Ra-Rasputin, Russia's greatest love machine,
G   D   A   E
It was a shame how he carried on.

RIVERS OF BABYLON
Boney M.

Chor: Mmmm (G / G / D / G)

                        G
By the rivers of Babylon there we sat down.
             D   G
Yeah we wept when we remembered Zion.
             D   G
Yeah we wept when we remembered Zion.

                        G   C   G
When the wicked carried us away in captiviby requiring of us a song.
                                        D
G
Now how shall we sing the Lord's song in a strange land?
                                     D G
Now how shall we sing the Lord's song in a strange land?)

          G   D   G   D
Let the words of our mouths and the meditations of our hearts
   G   D7   G
be acceptable in thy sight here tonight.
   G   D7   G
be acceptable in thy sight here tonight.

By the rivers of Babylon...

BROWN GIRL IN THE RING
Boney M

G
Brown girl in the ring, tra la la la la,
        D7
there's a brown girl in the ring, tra la la la la la.
 G
Brown girl in the ring, tra la la la la,
              D7   G
she looks like a sugar in the plum, plum, plum.

  G
Show me a motion, tra la la la la,
     D7
come on, show me a motion, tra la la la la la,
 G
show me a motion, tra la la la la,
         D7   G
she looks like a sugar in a plum, plum, plum.

G   D7   G
Old head water run dry, nowhere to wash my clothes.
G   D7   G
Old head water run dry, got nowhere to wash my clothes.
G   D7   G
I remember one saturday night, we had fried fish and Johnny cakes.
G   D7   G
I remember one saturday night, we had fried fish and Johnny cakes,
     D7 G   D7
dang-adang, dang-a-dang

NEIL DIAMOND

SONG SUNG BLUE
(Neil Diamond)

C   G
Song sung blue everybody knows one
                                    C
Song sung blue everybody grows one
       C7   F
Me and You are subject to the blues now and then
   G
But when you take the blues and make a song
                 C
 you sing them out again
         Dm   G7
Sing them out again
C   G
Song sung blue weepin like a willow
                          C   C7
Song sung blue sleepin on my pillow
C7   F
Funny thing but you can sing it with a cry in your voice
  G
And before you know it start to feelin good,
          C
You simply got no choice

SWEET CAROLINE
Neil Diamond

Intro Chords: E E E E

A   D
Where it began I can't begin to know it
A   E
But then I know it's going strong
A   D
Was in the spring, and spring became a summer
A   E
Who'd have believe you'd come along

Chorus
A   Amaj7   (Am7 002213)
Hands   touching hands
E   D   E
Reaching out touching me touching you

A   D   E
Sweet Caroline Good times never seemed so good
A   D   E
I'm inclined to believe there never would
D Dbm Bm
But now I'm….

Look at the night and it don't seem so lonely
We fill it up with only two
And when I hurt Hurting runs off my shoulder
How can I hurt when holding you
                              Chorus

CRACKLIN' ROSIE
Neil Diamond

[D]Cracklin' Rosie, get on board

We're gonna ride till there ain't no more to [G]go

Taking it slow Lord, don't you know
[Em]]ave me a time with a poor man's [A]lady
[D]Hitchin' on a twilight train

Ain't nothing there that I care to take a[G]long

Maybe a song To sing when I want
[Em]Don't ned to say please to no man for a [A7]happy [D]tune

CHORUS
[D]Oh, I l[G]ove my [A]Rosie c[D]hild
[Db]Oh, I l[Gb]ove my [Ab]Rosie c[Db]hild
[D]She got the [G]way to [A]make me[D] happy
[Db]She got the [Gb]way to [Ab]make me[Db] happy
[D]You and[G] me, we[A] go in [D]style
[Db]You and[Gb] me, we[Ab] go in [Db]style
[Em]
[Ebm]Cracklin' Rosie you're a store-bought woman
You make me sing like a guitar hummin'
So hang on to me, girl
Our song keeps runnin' [Ab]on
Play it now
Play it now
Play it now, my baby

KENNY ROGERS

THE GAMBLER

```
G                              C                    G
On a warm summer's evenin' on a train bound for nowhere
                                                   D
I met up with the gambler we were both too tired too sleep
  G                         C                    G
so we took turns a starin' out the window at the darkness '
     C     G     D       G
til boredom over took us and he began to speak.
    G                              C              G
He said, Son I've made a life out of reading peoples faces,
   C               G                           D
 and knowing what their cards were by the way they held
their eyes.
   G                         C                  G
And if you don't mind my sayin I can see you're out of aces,
   C        G       D            G
for a taste of your whiskey I'll give you some advice.
   G                        C                      G
So I handed him my bottle and he drank down my last
swallow.
                                G             D
Then he bummed a cigarette and asked me for a light.
     G                        C                G
And the night got deathly quiet, and his face lost all
expression
    C                        G           D           G
"If you're gonna play the game, boy ya gotta learn to play it
right...
```

CHORUS
```
G             G            C              G
You got to know how to hold 'em, know when to fold 'em,
C           G                        D
 know when to walk away and know when to run.
```

THE GAMBLER

*   G   C   G*
You never count your money when you're sittin' at the table.
*   C   G   D   G*
There'll be time enough for countin' when the dealin's done.

A   D   A
Every gambler knows that the secret to survivin' is knowin'
                      E
what to throw away and knowin' what to keep
     A   D   A
Cause every hands a winner and every hands a loser
    D   A   E   A
and the best that you can hope for is to die in your sleep.
A
And when he'd finished speakin',
 D   A
he turned back toward the window,
                              E
crushed out his cigarette and faded off to sleep.
  A   D   A
 And somewhere in the darkness the gambler he broke even
 D   A   E   A
but in his final words I found an ace that I could keep.

CHORUS

*   A*
You got to know when to hold 'em,
D   A
know when to fold 'em,
D   A   E
know when to walk away, and know when to run.
*   A E   A   D   A*
You never count your money when you're sittin' at the table.
*   D   A E   A*
There'll be time enough for countin' when the dealin's done.

LUCILLE

  C
In a bar in Toledo across from the depot,
....G7
on a bar stool she took off her ring.
   Dm   G7
I thought I'd get closer, so I walked on over,
 Dm   G7   C
I sat down and asked her, her name.
 C
When the drinks finally hit her, she said, I'm no quitter
              C7   F
But I finally quit living on dreams.
     G7
I'm hungry for laughter and here ever after
                         C
I'm after what ever the other life brings."

CHORUS
C   F
You picked a fine time to leave me Lucille,
                                     C
with four hungry children and a crop in the field.
F
I've had some bad times lived through some sad times
                               C
but this time your hurtin won't heal.
             G7   *C*
You picked a fine time to leave me Lucille.

REUBEN JAMES
(K. Rogers)

   D   A7   D   G   D
In my song you live again and the phrases that I rhyme
    A7   D
Are just the footsteps out of time
   G   D   A7   D
From the time when I knew you, Reuben James
     D
Reuben James, all the folks around Madison County
      A7
Cussed your name
   G   D
You're just a no-account, sharecropping colored man
 A7   D
Who'd steal anything he can
   G   D   A7   D
And everybody laid the blame on Reuben James

CHORUS:
  G   D
Reuben James, for you still walk the furthest field of my mind
  G
Faded shirt, your weathered brow
            D
Your caloused hands upon the plow
       C   D
I loved you then and I love you now, Reuben James

Flora Grey, the gossip of Madison County died with child
And although your skin was black
You were the one that didn't turn your back
On the hungry white child with no name Reuben James

JOHNNY CASH

BIG RIVER
Johnny Cash

```
   G                  C                G
Now I taught the weeping willow how to cry,
              G7            A7              D7
And I showed the clouds how to cover up a clear blue sky.
   G              G7                 C7
And the tears that I cried for that woman are gonna flood you Big River.
   G        D7  G   D7       G
Then I'm gonna sit right here until I die.
```

I met her accidentally in St. Paul (Minnesota).
And it tore me up ev'ry time I heard her drawl, Southern drawl.
Then I heard my dream was back downstream cavortin' in Davenport,
And I followed you, Big River, when you called.

Then you took me to St. Louis later on (down the river).
A freighter said she's been here but she's gone, boy, she's gone.
I found her trail in Memphis, but she just walked up the block.
She raised a few eyebrows and then she went on down alone.

Now, won't you batter down by Baton Rouge, River Queen, roll it on.
Take that woman on down to New Orleans, New Orleans.
Go on, I've had enough; dump my blues down in the gulf.
She loves you, Big River, more than me.

BOY NAMED SUE
Shel Silverstein by Johnny Cash

G
My daddy left home when I was three
   C
And he didn't leave much to Ma and me
   D   G
Just this old guitar and an empty bottle of booze.
G
Now, I don't blame him cause he run and hid
                  C
But the meanest thing that he ever did
   D   G
Was before he left, he went and named me 'Sue.'

Well, he must o' thought that is was quite a joke
And it got a lot of laughs from a' lots of folk,
It seems I had to fight my whole life through.
Some gal would giggle and I'd get red
And some guy'd laugh and I'd bust his head,
I tell ya, life ain't easy for a boy named 'Sue.'

Well, I grew up quick and I grew up mean,
 My fist got hard and my wits got keen,
I'd roam from town to town to hide my shame.
 But I made me a vow to the moon and stars
That I'd search the honky-tonks and bars
And kill that man that give me that awful name.

Well, it was Gatlinburg in mid-July
And I just hit town and my throat was dry,
 I thought I'd stop and have myself a brew.
 At an old saloon on a street of mud,
 There at a table, dealing stud,
 Sat the dirty, mangy dog that named me 'Sue.'

Well, I knew that snake was my own sweet dad
From a worn-out picture that my mother'd had,

HOME OF THE BLUES
Johnny Cash

LEADIN   A B7 E E   A A E E B7 B7 E E

```
 A           B7             E
Just around the corner there's heartache—
 A           B7             E
Down the street that losers use
 A           B7                E
If you can wade in through the teardrops,
 A              B7          E
You'll find me at the Home of the Blues
```

I walk and cry while my heartbeat
Keeps time with the drag of my shoes
The sun never shines through this window of mine
It's dark at the Home of the Blues
```
        A                     E
Oh, but the place is filled with the sweetest mem'ries
 B7             E
Mem'ries so sweet that I cry—
 A                     E
Dreams that I've had left me  feelin' so bad,
 F#7                   B7        (F#7 043210)
I just want to give up and lay down and die—
```

So if you've just lost your sweetheart,
And it seems there's no good way to choose
Come along with me, mis'ry loves company
You're welcome at the Home of the Blues

BALLAD OF A TEENAGE QUEEN
by Marcel Veltman, Johnny Cash

LEADIN F C F C F C G C
```
 F          C         F     C
```
Dream on dream on teenage queen
```
    F       C      G     C
```
The prettiest girl we've ever seen
```
C          F      C
```
There's a story in this town
```
            G         C
```
Of the prettiest girl around
```
              F     C
```
Golden hair and eyes of blue
```
              G       C
```
How these eyes could blush off you
```
              G     C
```
(How these eyes could blush off you, aaahaaahaa....)
```
F              C
```
Boys hung round her by the score
```
            G         C
```
But she loved the boy next door
```
            G    C
```
Who worked at the candy store

FIVE FEET HIGH AND RISIN'
John Cash

No Chord
How high's the water, Mama?
A
Two feet high and risin'.
A
How high's the water, Papa?
A
Two feet high and risin'.

      A
We can make it to the road, in a homemade boat,
      A
That's the only thing we got left that'll float,
   E
It's / already over all the wheat and the oats,
E -   A
Two feet high and risin'.

C
How high's the water, Mama?
C
Three feet high and risin'
C
How high's the water, Papa?
C
Three feet high and risin'.
     C
Well, the hives are gone, I've lost my bees.
  C
The chickens are sleepin' in the willow trees.

G
Cow's in water up past her knees,
G   -   C
Three feet high and risin'.

D
How high's the water, Mama?
D
Four feet high and risin'.
D
How high's the water, Papa?
D
Four feet high and risin'.
D
Hey, come look through the window pane,
    A
The bus is comin', gonna take us to the train
A
Looks like we'll be blessed with a little more rain,
A   -   D
Four feet high and risin'

E
How high's the water, Mama?
E
Five feet high and risin'.
E
How high's the water, Papa?
E
Five feet high and risin'.
      E
Well, the / rails are washed out north of town,
E

We gotta head for higher ground,
    B
We can't come back, till the water comes down,
B   -   E
Five feet high and risin'.
      E
Well, it's five feet high and risin'.

GET RHYTHM
by Johnny Cash

E
Hey GET RHYTHM when you get the blues
        A   E
Hey get rhythm when you get the blues
Yes a jumpy rhythm makes you feel so fine
It'll shake all the trouble from your worried mind
   A   B7   E
Get rhythm when you get the blues
E
Little shoeshine boy never gets low down
But he's got the dirtiest job in town
Bendin' low at the peoples' feet
On the windy corner of the dirty street
Well I asked him while he shined my shoes
How'd he keep from gettin' the blues
He grinned as he raised his little head
Popped a shoeshine rag and then he said
CHORUS
GET RHYTHM when you get the blues
Hey get rhythm when you get the blues
It only costs a dime just a nickel a shoe
Does a million dollars worth of good for you
Get rhythm when you get the blues
 [E]
Well I sat down to listen to the shoeshine boy
And I thought I was gonna jump for joy
Slapped on the shoe polish left and right
He took a shoeshine rag and he held it tight
He stopped once to wipe the sweat away
I said you're a mighty little boy to be-a workin' that way
He said I like it with a big wide grin
Kept on a poppin' and he said again

GUESS THINGS HAPPEN THAT WAY
(Johnny Cash)

A   D
Well, you ask me if I'll forget my baby
A   D
I guess I will some day
A   E   A (E)
I don't like it but I guess things happen that way

 A   A
You ask me if I'll get along
A   D
I guess I will some way
A   E   A (E)
I don't like it but I guess things happen that way

CHORUS:
D   A   E   A   D
God gave me that girl to lean on, then he put me on my own
D   A   E   A
Heaven help me be a man and have the strength to stand alone
A   E   A (E)
I don't like it but I guess things happen that way

You ask me if I'll miss her kisses
I guess I will every day
I don't like it but I guess things happen that way

You ask me if I'll find another
I don't know, I can't say
I don't like it but I guess things happen that way

TENNESSEE STUD
(Johnny Cash)

A
Back about eighteen and twenty-five
G
I left Tennessee very much alive
A
I never would've made it through the Arkansas mud
E   A
If I hadn't been riding on the Tennessee Stud

A
Had some trouble with my sweetheart's Pa
G
One of her brothers was a bad outlaw
A
I wrote a letter to my Uncle Fudd
E   A
And I rode away on the Tennessee Stud

A   G   A
|The Tennessee Stud was long and lean
D   C   E
|The color of the sun and his eyes were green
A
|He had the nerve and he had the blood
E   A
|There never was a horse like Tennessee Stud

RING OF FIRE -
June Carter, Merle Kilgore (JOHNNY CASH

INTRO: G   C G   C
```
 G          C           G
```
Love Is A Burning Thing
```
             C    G
```
And It Makes A Firery Ring
```
      C   G
```
Bound By Wild Desire
```
            C        G
```
I Fell Into A Ring Of Fire

CHORUS:
```
D            C              G
```
I Fell Into A Burning Ring Of Fire
```
         D
```
I Went Down, Down, Down
```
         C         G
```
And The Flames Went Higher

And It Burns, Burns, Burns
```
     C     G
```
The Ring Of Fire
```
     C     G
```
The Ring Of Fire

Repeat INTRO Twice
Repeat CHORUS

FOLSOM PRISON BLUES
(Johnny Cash)

G
I hear the train a comin', it's rollin' round the bend,
                              G
and I ain't seen the sunshine since I don't know when.
C   G
I'm stuck at Folsom prison and time keeps draggin' on.
    D7   G
But that train keeps rollin' on down to San Antone.

When I was just a baby my mama told me son,
Always be a good boy; don't ever play with guns.
But I shot a man in Reno just to watch him die,
When I hear that whistle blowin', I hang my head and cry.

I bet there's rich folks eatin' in a fancy dining ca.
They're prob'ly drinkin' coffee and smoking big cigars.
But I know I had it comin', I know I can't be free,
But those people keep a-movin', and that's what tortures me.

Well, if they freed me from this prison,
if that railroad train was mine,
I bet I'd move on over a little farther down the line,
Far from Folsom prison, that's where I want to stay.
And I'd let that lonesome whistle blow my blues away.

TENNESSEE FLAT TOP BOX

INTRO C   F   C

C   G7
In a little cabaret in south Texas border town

                                                         C
Sat a boy and his guitar and the people came from all around

                                      G
And all the girls from there to Austin were slipping away from home

                                  C
and putting in hock to take a trip to go

    G
and listen to the little dark haired boy

                             C
who played the Tennesse flat top box

              F
And he would play

INTERLUDE   C   F   C   F   F   C

Well, he couldn't ride or wrangle and he never cared to make a dime
But give him his guitar and he'd be happy all the time
And all the girls from nine to ninety
Were snapping fingers, tapping toes and begging him, "don't stop"
And hypnotized, and fascinated by the
Little dark haired boy who played Tennessee flat top box.
And he would play

DADDY SANG BASS
(Johnny Cash)

```
INTRO G        D7            G
```

D7   G7   C   G
I remember when I was a lad, times were hard and things were bad;
D7   G   D   A7 D7
But there's a silver lining behind every cloud.
  G   G7
Just poor people that's all we were,
      C   G
 tryin' to make a livin' out of black and dirt
D7   G   D7   G   C   G
We'd get together in a family circle, singin' loud
D7   G   G7
Daddy sang bass mama sang tenor
      C   G
me and little brother would join right in there singin'
        D   A7   D7
Seems to help a troubled soul
        G   G7   C   G
One of these days and it won't be long, I'll rejoin them in a song;
          D7   G   C   G
I'm gonna join the family circle at the throne
D7   G   G7   C   G
No the circle won't be broken bye and bye, Lord, bye and bye:
D7   G   C
Daddy'll sing bass, mama'll sing tenor, me and little brother
will join right in there singin seems to help a troubled soul
One of these days and it won't be long,
 I'll rejoin them in a song; I'm gonna join the family circle at the

I WALK THE LINE
(Johnny Cash)

A   E   A
I keep a close watch on this heart of mine.
           E   A
I keep my eyes wide open all the time.
          D   A
I keep the ends out for the time that binds.
              E   A
Because you're mine I walk the line.

I find it very easy to be true.
I find myself alone when each day is through.
Yes, I'll admit that I'm a fool for you.
Because you're mine I walk the line.

As sure as night is dark and day is light.
I keep you on my mind both day and night.
And happiness I've known proves that it's right.
Because you're mine I walk the line.

You've got a way to keep me on your side.
You give me cause for love that I can't hide.
For you I know Id' even try to turn the tide.
Because you're mine I walk the line.

I keep a close watch on this heart of mine.
I keep my eyes wide open all the time.
I keep the ends out for the tie that binds.
Because you're mine I walk the line.

WESTERN COUNTRY MIX

ABILENE

`C      E     E7      F     C      A7`
Abilene, Abelene Prettiest town I ever seen
`D7              G7`
Folks out there don't treart you mean
`     C    C7 F Fm  C`
In Abelene, my Ableline

`C      E     E7`
Sit alone erery night
`F    F# Am      C      A7`
Watch the train run out of sight
`D7              G7`
Don't I wish they were carrying me to
` C       C7 F Fm C Ab G7`
Abilene, my Abilene

`C           E          E7`
Crowded city aint nothing free
`F     F#dim     C     A7`
Aint nothing in this town for me
`D7              G7`
Don't I wish that I could be in
` C       C7 F Fm C Ab G7`
Abilene, my Abilene

Fm 003111

ACT NATURALLY

G   C
They're gonna put me in the movies.
G   D7
They're gonna make a big star out of me.
         G   C
We'll make a film about a man that's sand and lonely,
         D7   G
 and all I gotta do is act naturally.
         D7   G
Well I bet you I'm gonna be a big star.
         D7   G
Might win an Oscar, you can never tell.
         D7   G   A7   D7
The movies gonna make me a big star cause I can play the part so well.
         G   C
Well, I hope you come and see me in the movies,
G   D7
Then I'll know that you will plainly see the
 G   C
biggest fool that ever hit the big time,
D7   G
and all I got to do is act naturally.

We'll make the scene about a man that's sad and lonely,
And beggin' down upon his bended knee.
I'll play the part but I won't need rehearsin'
All I have to do is act naturally.

Well, I hope you come and see me in the movies,
Then I'll know that you will plainly see the biggest fool that
ever hit the big time, and all I got to do is act naturally.

AMANDA

C   F   C
I've held it all inward, Lord knows I've tried.
                         G7   C
It's an awful awakening in a country boy's life.
                             F   C
To look in the mirror in total surprise at the hair on
     G7   C
your shoulders and the age in your eyes.

CHORUS
C   F   C
Amanda light of my life, fate should have made you
   G7   C
a gentleman's wife.
C   F   C
Amanda light of my life fate should have made you
   G7   C
 a gentleman's wife.

Well the measure of people don't understand
The pleasures of a life in a hillbilly band.
I got my first guitar when I was fourteen.
Now I'm crowding thirty and still wearin' jeans.
CHORUS

ON THE ROAD AGAIN
Willie Nelson

E   G#m
On the road again, just can't get wait to get on the road again.
                          F#m   (F#m 114222)
I find love is makin' music with my friends. (G#m 466444)
   A   B   E
And I can't wait to get on the road again.

On the road again, going places that I've never been.
Seein' things that I may never see again.
And I can't wait to get on the road again.

    A
On the road again, I

                          E
Like a band of gypsies we go down the highway
             A
We're the best of friends, insisting that the world keep
E   B
 turnin' our way, and our way

On the road again, just can't get wait to get on the road again.
I find love is makin' music with my friends.
And I can't wait to get on the road again.

guitar solo x2 verses

HAVE I TOLD YOU LATELY THAT I LOVE YOU

C   G7
Have I told you lately that I love you?
                              C
Could I tell you once again somehow?
      F   C
Have I told with all my heart and soul how I adore you?
      G7   C
Well darling I'm telling you now.
C   C7   F   C
This heart would break in two if you refuse me.
      G7   C
I'm no good without you anyhow.
      C7   F   C
 Dear, have I told you lately that I love you?
      G7   C   F G
Well, darling I'm telling you now.

Have I told you lately how I miss you.
When the stars are shining in the sky?
Have I told you why the nights are long when you're not with me?
Well, darling, I'm telling you now.

Have I told you lately when I'm sleeping?
Ev'ry dream I dream is you somehow?
Have I told you I'd like to share my love forever?
Well, darling, I'm telling you now.

HEARTACHES BY THE NUMBER

C   F
Heartache number one was when you left me
     G7   C
I never knew that I could hurt this way
                                              F
And heartache number two was when you came back again
G7   C
You came back and never meant to stay

           C
Now I've got heart aches by the number
F
Troubles by the score
G7
Every day you love me less
                 C
Each day I love you more
       C
Yes I've got heartaches by the number

A love that I can't win
    G7
But the day that I stop counting
                      C
That's the day my world will end

Heartache number three was when you called me
And said that you were coming back to stay
With hopefull heart I waited for your knock on the door
I waited but you must have lost your way

JAMBALAYA (ON THE BAYOU)

INTRO C   Am   G7   C

C   G7
Goodbye, Joe, me gotta go, me oh, my oh.
                                 C
Me gotta go pole the pirogue down the bayou.
                            G7
My Yvonne, the sweetest one, me o, my oh.
G7   C
Son of a gun, we'll have big fun on the bayou.

CHORUS
    C   G7
Jambalaya and a crawfish pie and fillet gumbo,
                          C
caus to night I'm gonna see my cheramio,
                          G7
pick guitar, fill fruit jar and be Gayo
                                      C
Son of a gun, we'll have big fun on the bayou.

Thi bo daux, Fontaineaux, the place is buzzin.
Kinfolk come to see Yvonne by the dozen.
Dress in style and go hog wild, me oh, my oh.
CHORUS
Settle down far from town, get me a pirogue.
And I'll catch all the fish in the bayou.
Swap my mon to buy Yvonne what we need-o.
CHORUS

KISS AN ANGEL GOOD MORNIN

      G   G7   C
When ever I chance to meet some old friends on the street
    D7   G
They wonder how does a man get to be this way
G   G7   C
I've always got a smiling face, any time and any place
   D
 and everytime they ask me why
             G
I just smile and say

CHORUS
G   D7
you've got to kiss an angel good morning
  C   G   C
 and let her know you think about her when you're gone
                      D7
Kiss an angel good morning
  C   G
and love her like the devil when you get back home.

Well people may try to guess the secret of happiness,
But some of them never learn it's a simple thing.
The secret I'm speakin of is a woman and man in love,
And the answer is in the son that I always sing.
CHORUS

LUCKENBACH, TEXAS

```
          G              D                    G            C
The only two things in life that make it worth livin' are guitars
                          D      G
 that tune good and firm feelin women.
C                              G
I don't need my name in the marquee lights;
   C              D7              G
I got my song and I got you with me tonight.
C                   D             G
Maybe it's time we got back to the basics of love.
```

CHORUS

```
                  G                                      C
Let's go to Luckenbach Texas, with Waylon and Willie and the
boys
        D                                                G
This successful life we're livin got us feudin' like the Hatfields and
McCoys
 G                                G7
Between Hank William's pain songs and Newberry's train songs
          C               Am
and "Blue eyes cryin' in the rain."
          D                                        G   Am  D
Out in Luckenbach, Texas, ain't nobody feelin' no pain.
     G
So, baby let's sell your diamond ring,
  Am7            D7             G
buy some boots and faded jeans and go away.
                          Am7      D        G
This coat and tie is choking me, In your society you cry all day.
                          G7              C
We've been so busy keeping up with the Jones' four car garage,
          Am
and we're still buildin' on,
  C      G        D              G
Maybe it's time we got back to the basics of love.
```

RUBY DON'T TAKE YOUR LOVE TO TOWN

G   C   Dm7   G
You have painted up your lips and rolled and curled your tinted hair.
C   Dm7   G
Ruby are you contemplating going out somewhere?
     Dm   G7   Em
The shadows on the wall tell me the sun is going down.

CHORUS
     C G Am7 G F C Dm7   G7   C
Oh, Ru……….by…………., don't take your love to town.
     Dm7   G7   F   C
For it wasn't me that started that old crazy Asian war
     Dm7   F   G
but I was proud to go and do my patriotic chores.
     Dm7   G7   Em
Oh, I know, Ruby, that I'm not the man I used to be,
     C G Am7 G F C Dm7   G7   C
but, Ru………by……….., I still need your company.

It's hard to love a man whose legs are bet and paralyzed.
And the wants and need of a woman your age Ruby, I realize.
But it won't be long, I've heard them say until I'm not around.
Oh, Ruby, don't take your love to town.

She's leaving now 'cause I just heard the slamming of the door.
The way I know I've heard it slam one hundred times before.
And if I could move I'd get my gun and put her in the ground.
Oh, Ruby, don't take your love to town.
For God's sake turn around.

OKIE FROM MUSKOGEE

   G
We don't smoke marijuana in Muskogee and
                     D7
we don' take our trips on LSD
D7
And we don't burn our draft cards down on Main Street,
G
but we like living right and being free.

CHORUS
.........G
And I'm proud to be an Okie from Muskogee.
                         D7
A place where even squares can have a ball.

We still wave Ol' Glory down at the court house
                       G
White lightning's still the biggest thrill of all

We don't make a party out of loving
But we like holding hands and pitching woo
We don't let our hair grow long and shaggy
Like hippies out in San Francisco do
CHORUS
Leather boots are still in style if a man needs footwear
Beads and Roman sandals won't be seen
Football's still the roughest thing on campus
And the kids here still respect the college dean
CHORUS

BOBBY McGEE

C
Busted flat in Batton Rouge

Heading for the trains
                      G7
Feelin' nearly faded as my jeans

Bobby thumbed a diesel down, just before it rained
                         C
Took us all the way to New Orleans

I took my harpoon out of my dirty old bandana
                              F
And was blowin' sad while Bobby sang the blues

With them windshield wipers slappen' time
C
And Bobby clappin hands with mine
        G7   C
We finely sang up every song that driver knew
F   C
Freedoms just another word for nothing left to lose
 G7   C
Nothing ain't worth nothing but it's free
  F   C
Feeling good was easy lord when Bobby sang the blues
 G7
Feeling good was good enough for me
                           C
Good enough for me and Bobby McGee

KING OF THE ROAD

C   Dm7   G7   C
Trailer for sale or rent, Rooms to let fifty cents
            Dm7   G7
No phone, no pool, no pets, I aint got no cigarrettes
         C   Dm7   G7
C
Ah but two hours of pushing broom buy an eight by twelve four bit room
            F   G7   C
I'm a man of means by no means   King of the road

C   Dm7   G7   C
Third box car midnight train, Destination Bangor Maine
            Dm7   G7
Old worn-out suit and shoes, I don't pay no union dues
           C   Dm7   G7   C
I smoke old stogies I have found, Short but not too big and round
            F   G7   C
I'm a man of means by no means   King of the road

C   F   G7   C
I know every engineer on every train, All of the children all of the names
                   F
And every hand-out in every town
            G   G7
And every lock that ain't locked when no one's around
I sing trailer for sale or rent, rooms to let fifty cents.
No phone, no pool, no pets, I ain't got no cigarettes.
Ah but two hours of pushing broom buys a eight by twelve four bit room.
I'm a man of means by no means. King of the road.

SIXTEEN TONS

Em
Some people say a man is made out of mud

A poor mans made out of muscle and blood
                                          Am
Muscle and blood and skin and bone
  C   Em
A mind that's weak and back that's strong
CHORUS
          Em
You load sixteen tons what do you get?

Another day older and deeper in debt
                                    Am
Saint Peter don't you call me cause I cant go
  Em
I owe my sole to the company store
B7   Em   B7   Em

I was born one mornin' when the sun didn't shine
I picked up my shovel and I walked to the mine
I loaded sixteen tons of number nine coal
And the straw boss said, "Well a bless my soul".
CHORUS
I was born one mornin' it was drizzling rain
Fightin' and trouble are my middle name
I was raised in a cane brake by an ole mama lion
Ain't no high toned woman make me walk the line
CHORUS
If you see me comin' better step aside,
A lotta men didn't, a lotta men died
One fist of iron the other of steel
If the right don't get you, then the left one will.
CHORUS

Oh LORD IT'S HARD TO BE HUMBLE
(Mac Davis)

CHORUS
G   D
Oh Lord it's hard to be humble, when your perfect in every way
                                                           G
I can't wait to look in a mirror, As I get better looking each day
G   C
To know me is to love me, I must be a helluva man
                         D   G
Oh lord it's hard to be humble. But I'm doin' the best that I can

I used to have a girlfriend,
But she just couldn't compete
With all these loved starved women,
who keep clammering at my feet
Well I prob'/y could find me another
But I guess they're all in awe of me
Who cares, I never get lonesome
'cause I treasure my own company
CHORUS

I guess you say I'm a loner
A cowboy outlaw tough and proud
I could have lots of friends if I want to
But then I wouldn't stand out in a crowd
Some say I am egotistical
Hell I don't even know what that means
It must have something to do
With the way I fill out my skintight blue jeans
CHORUS

PUT ANOTHER LOG ON THE FIRE
(Shel Silverstein)

CHORUS
G
Put another log on the fire,
G   D
cook me up some bacon and some beans.
And go out to the car and change the tire,
*   G*
wash my socks and sew my old blue jeans.
Come on, baby, you can
fill my pipe and then go fetch my slippers,
*   C*
and boil me up another pot of tea,
*   G*
Then put another log on my fire, babe,
* D   G*
and come and tell me why you`re leaving me.

Oh, don`t I let you wash the car on Sunday,
don`t I warn you when you`re getting fat.
Ain`t I gonna take you fishing with me some day,
well, a man can`t love a woman more than that.
Ain`t I always nice to your kid sister,
don`t I take her driving every night.
So sit here at my feet,
`cause I like you when you`re sweet,
and you know it ain`t feminine to fight. So...
CHORUS

SUNDOWN
(Gordon Lightfoot)

```
E                             A
I can see her lying there in a satan dress
B7                               E
In a room where you do what you don't confess
E             A
Sundown you'd better take care
         D                      E
If I find you've been creeping down my back stair
```

She's been looking like a queen in a sailors dream
And she wont always say what she really means
Sometimes I think it's a shame
When I get feeling better when I feeling no pain
When I get feeling better when I feeling no pain

I can picture every move that a man could make
Getting lost in your loving is your first mistake
Sundown you'd better take care
If I find you've been creeping down my back stair

Sometimes I think it's a sin
When I feel like I'm winning when I'm losing again
Can see her looking back in her faded years
She's a hard looking woman got me feelin mean
Sundown you'd better take care
If I find you've been creeping down my back stair

SHENADOAH

    F
The old Mizou she's a mighty river
  Dm   Am
 Way you rolling river
    F   Dm
The Indians camp along her border
  F   Dm   Am   C7   F
Away were bound a way across the wide Missouri

The white man loved an Indian maiden,
Way your rolling river
With notions his canoe was laden
Away were bound a way across the wide Missouri

Oh Shenandoah, I love your daughter
Way you rolling river
I'll take her cross your rollin' river
Away were bound a way across the wide Missouri

The chief disdained the traders dollar
Way you rolling river
My daughter you shall never follow
Away were bound a way across the wide Missouri

He told the chief that firewater
Way you rolling river
And cross that river he stole his daughter
Away were bound a way across the wide Missouri

Fare you well, I'm bound to leave you
Way you rolling river
Oh, Shenandoah I'll not deceive you
Away were bound a way across the wide Missouri

STORMS NEVER LAST
(Waylon Jennings)

CHORUS:
```
   G              C/G
Storms never last do they baby
   D              G
Bad times will pass with the winds
                    C/G
Your hand in mine steals the thunder
   D          G
You make the sun want to shine
```

Verse :
```
 G                      C/G
Oh, I followed you down so many roads...baby
   D                           G
I picked wild flowers and sung you soft sweet songs
                                          C/G
And ever road we took God knows our search was for the truth
         D                     G
And the storm brewin' now won't be the last
```

CHORUS.
```
   G              C/G
Storms never last do they Jessie
   D              G
Bad times will pass with the winds
 G                  C/G
Your hand in mine steals the thunder
   D          G
You make the sun want to shine
```

JUST AN OLD HIPPY Bellamy Brothers

A
He turned thirty-five last Sunday,
D   A
And his hair is bouncin' grey
But he still ain't changed his lifestyle,
                   E
He likes it better the (old way.
    D
So he grows a little garden in the
A
backyard by the fence
        D
He's consumin' what he's growin'
    A   E
Now-a-days in self-defense
        A
He get's out there in the twilight zone some
D   A
times, when it just don't make no sense.
CHORUS
            D
'Cause he's an OLD HIPPY, and he
A   D
don't know what to do, should he hang on to the old
            A   E
or should he grab onto the new
        D   A
He's and OLD HIPPY, this new life just ain't the stuff

He ain't tryin' to change nobody,
        E   A
he's just tryin' real hard to adjust.

LET ME BE THERE

CHORUS

D
Let me be there in your morning
      G
Let me be there in your night
       D
Let me change whatever's wrong
         A
And make it right, make it right
   D
Let me take you through that wonderland
  G
That only I can share
   D   *A*
All I ask you ooh ooh ohh
    D
Is let me be there

D
Watching you grow
              G   E
And going through changes in your life
                         A
That's all I know I'll always want to be there
             D   G   D
Whenever you feel you need a friend to lean on here I am
         A   D
Whenever you call you know I'll be there

CHORUS

RHINESTONE COWBOY

C
I've been walkin' these streets so long, Singin' the same old song

                                                  G
I know every crack in these dirty sidewalks of Broadway
    F
Where hustles the name of the game

                                                              C
And nice guys get washed away like the snow and the rain
           G   F   C
There's been a load of compromising on the road to my arising
  F   G
But I'm gonna be where the lights are shining on me

CHORUS

                C
Like a rhinestone cowboy riding out on a horse,
              G
in a star spangled rodeo
  C
Like a rhinestone cowboy getting cards and letters
                         G
From people I don't even know
  F   C
And offers come over the phone

C
Well I really don't mind the rain,
And a smile can hide all the pain
But your down when you're riding the train
         G
That's taking the long way
 F
And I dream of the thing's I'll do

                                               C
With a subway token and a dollar tucked my shoe

WALK ON BY

```
C           F        G7                    C
```
If I see you tomorrow on some street in town
```
        F       G7       C
```
Pardon me if I don't say hello
```
  C            F
```
I belong to another
```
        G7            C       F
```
It wouldn't look so good to know someone
```
   G7              C
```
I'm not supposed to know

CHORUS

```
              C
```
Just walk on by
```
              G7
```
Wait on the corner
```
    F                    G7               C
```
I love you but we're strangers when we meet
```
                              G7
```
Just walk on by, wait on the corner
```
    F                   G7              C
```
I love you but we're strangers when we meet

In a dimly lit corner
In a place outside of town
Tonight we'll try to say goodbye again
But I know it's not over
I'll call tomorrow night
I can't let you go
So why pretend

CHORUS

SUMMER WAGES

Intro C F C G C

    C   F
Never hit seventeen When you play against the dealer
    C   G
You know that the odds won't ride with you
    C   F
Never leave your woman alone With your friends around to steal her
        C   G   C
She'll be gambled and gone, Like summer wages

And we'll keep rollin on, Till we get to Vancouver
And the lady that I love She's living there
Its been six long months. And more since I've seen her
Maybe she's gambled and gone. Like summer wages
CHORUS
    G   C
In all the beer parlors, all down along Main Street
    G   D
 The dreams of the season are spilled down on the floor
      G   C
All the big stands of timber wait there just for fallin'
    G   D G
The hookers stand watchfully waitin' by the door

I'm going to work on them towboats
With my slippery city shoes
Lord I swore I would never do that again
Through the great fog bound straights
Where the cedars stand waitin
I'll be lost and gone, Like summer wages
(CHORUS)
           G C   G C

Like summer wages, Summer Wages

DELLA AND THE DEALER
(Hoyt Axton)

   A
It was Della and a dealer and a dog named Jake,
   D
And a cat named Kalamazoo,
 C   F
Left the city in a pick-up truck.
     D   A
Gonna make some dreams come true.
   A
Yeah, they rolled out west where the wild sun sets,
       D
And the coyote bays at the moon.
 C   F
Della and a dealer and a dog named Jake,
   D   A
And a cat named Kalamazoo.
CHORUS
   A
If that cat could talk, what tales he'd tell,
   E
About Della and the Dealer and the dog as well.
                                    A
But the cat was cool, And he never said a mumblin' word.

Down Tucson way there's a small cafe,
Where they play a little cowboy tune.
And the guitar picker was a friend of mine,
By the name of Randy Boone.
Yeah, Randy played her a sweet love song,
And Della got a fire in her eye.
The Dealer had a knife and the dog had a gun,
And the cat had a shot of rye.

WOLVERTON MOUNTAIN

```
  D    A7   D                     A7
They say don't go on Wolverton Mountain
                         D
If you're looking for a wife
        A7    D                         A7
'Cause Clifton Clowers has a pretty young daughter
                                  D
He's mighty handy with a gun and a knife.
```

CHORUS:
```
          A7                    D
Her tender lips are sweeter than honey
          D7    E7              A    A7
And Wolver] ton  mountain protects her there
           D                A7
The bears and birds tell Clifton Clowers
                  D
If a stranger should enter there.
```

All of my dreams are on Wolverton Mountain
I want his daughter for my wife
I'll take my chances and climb that mountain
Though Clifton Clowers, might take my life.
CHORUS

I'm goin' up on Wolverton Mountain
It's too lonesome down here be-low
It's just not right to hide his daughter
From the one who loves her so.
CHORUS

WOLVERTON MOUNTAIN

LAST VERSE
        A7
But I don't care about Clifton Clowers
        D
I'm gonna climb up on his mountain
        A7
I'm gonna take the girl I love
     D
I don't] care about Clifton Clowers
        A7
I'm a gonna climb up on that mountain
     D
And I'll get the one I love [fade]
     A7
I don't care about Clifton Clowers....

Wolverton Mountain

IT'S A HEARTACHE

     C   Em
1. It's a heartache, nothing but a heartache,
         F   C   G
   hits you when it's too late, hits you when you're down.
     C   Em
   It's a fool's game, nothing but a fool's game,
       F   C   G
   standing in the cold rain, feeling like a clown.

     C   Em
2. It's a heartache, nothing but a heartache,
       F   C   G
   love him till your arms break, then he let's you down.

    F   G
It ain't right with love to share,
   Em   Am   G
when you find he doesn't care, for you.
   F   G
It ain't wise to need someone,
   Em   Am   G
as much as I depended on, you.

SILVER THREADS AND GOLDEN NEEDLES
Dolly Parton

I don't want your lonely mansions
With a tear in every room
All I want's the love you   promised
Beneath the haloed m   oon
Do you think I should be happy
With your money and your name
And drown myself in sorrow
While you play your cheatin' game

CHORUS
    C

Silver threads and golden needles
Cannot mend this heart of mine
And I dare not drown my sorrows
In the warm glow of your win ine
You can't buy my love with money
Cause I never was that kind
   G

Silver threads and golden needles
    D   G
Cannot mend this heart of mine

Silver threads and golden needles
Cannot mend this heart of mine
And I dare not drown my sorrows
In the warm glow of your win   e
You can't buy my love with money
Cause I never was that kind
Silver threads and golden needles
Cannot mend this heart of mine

THREE WHEELS ON MY WAGON
Christie Minstrels

G   D   G
Three wheels on my wagon,
    C   G   D
And I'm still rolling along
 G   C   G   C
The Cherokees are chasing me
 G   C G   C
Arrows fly, right on by
G   D   G
But I'm singing a happy song
CHORUS
I'm singing a higgity, haggity, hoggety, high
Pioneers, they never say die
A mile up the road there's a hidden cave
And we can watch those Cherokees
Go galloping by

Two wheels on my wagon, And I'm still rolling along
Them Cherokees are after me
Flaming spears, burn my ears
But I'm singing a happy song

One wheel on my wagon, And I'm still rolling along
Them Cherokees after me
I'm all in flames, at the reins
But I'm singing a happy song

No wheels on my wagon, So I'm not rolling along
The Cherokees captured me
They look mad, things look bad
But I'm singing a happy song

BLACK FLY

Wade Hemsworth

    C   *
'Twas early in the spring when I decide to go
    A   D
For to work up in the woods in North On-tar-i-o
  C
The unemployment office said they'd send me through
   A   D
To the Little Abi-tibi with the survey crew

CHORUS:
      A   *
And the black flies, the little black flies
C
Always the black fly, no matter where you go
  D
I'll die with the black fly a-picking my bones
                C * *   D A
In North On-tar-i-o-i-o, in North On-tar-i-o

Now the man, black Toby was the captain of the crew
And he said, "I'm gonna tell you boys what we're gonna do
They want to build a power dam and we must find a way
For to make the Little Ab flow around the other way"

So we survey to the east and we survey to the west
And we couldn't make our minds up how to do it best
Little Ab, Little Ab, what shall I do
For I'm all but goin' crazy on the survey crew

JOY TO THE WORLD (Hoyt Axton)

```
D                         C Db  D    (Db 003121)
Jerimiah was a bullfrog
D                         C Db  D
Was a good friend of mine
         D7              G      Bb6   (
Never understood a single word he said
     D         A7         D
But I helped him a drinkin' his wine
     G7             A7           D
Yes, he always had some mighty fine wine
```
Chorus:

If I were the king of the world,
Tell you what I'd do:
Throw away the cars and the bars and the wars,
And make sweet love to you.
Yes, I'd make sweet love to you.

Chorus.
You know I love the ladies,
Love to have my fun.
I'm a high night flyer and a rainbow rider,
A straight shootin' son-of-a-gun.

CARIBBEAN BEAT

SLOOP JOHN B

C
We come on the sloop John B My grandfather and me
                          G7
Around Nassau town we did roam
                CF   F
Drinking all night, Got into a fight
     C   G7   C
Well I feel so broke up, I want to go home

CHORUS
So hoist up the John B's sail, See how the mainsail sets
Call for the captain ashore, Let me go home, let me go home
I wanna go home, yeah yeah, Well I feel so broke up I wanna go home

The first mate he got drunk, And broke in the cap'n's trunk
The constable had to come and take him away
Sheriff john stone, Why don't you leave me alone, yeah yeah
Well I feel so broke up I wanna go home
CHORUS

JAMAICA FAREWELL

C   F
In Jamaica where hearts are light
     C G7   C
Where music has you dancing all night
C   F
A boy was walking along a pier
       C   G7 C
He sang a little song I still can hear
CHORUS
     C   Dm7
Oh so sad am I to say goodbye
G7   C
I'll come back no more will I cry
                Dm7
I hate to say fairwell Jamiaca today
      C   G7   C
Because the girl I love is here down Kingston way

In Jamaica where rum comes from
Eveybody dances hear the banjo strum
They sing calypso, we all take part
Yet I heard a song from a broken heart
CHORUS

In Jamaica you can play and fish
And the Yankee dollar buys you what you wish
I was so happy with everythinhg
And yet it made me sad when I heard him sing
CHORUS

LA BAMBA

INTRO C F G7   C F G7

```
C       F          G
```
Bai la bai la Bai la Bamba
```
C       F          G
```
Bai la bai la Bai la Bamba
```
        C        F         G
```
Seres si sl un a po ca de gracia
```
C       F       G              C       F       G
```
Una poca de gracia para nui para ti yari ba ya ri ba
```
C   F    G            C      F       G
```
A ya riba a riba por ti sere yo nosoy mari nero
```
C    F    G              C   F   G
```
Yo no soy mari nero por ti sere por ti sere

```
G     F   G         F    G
```
Bam ba Bamba Bam ba Bamba
```
       F    G         F    G
```
Bam ba Bamba Bam ba Bamba

MARIANNE

```
C                                    G7
Marianne oh Marianne Oh wont you marry me
                                        C
We can have a bamboo hut and brandy in the tea
C                                       F
Leave your fat old mama home she never will say yes
G7         C        G7     C
If mama don't know now, she can guess, my, my, yes
```

CHORUS
```
C           G       G7                           C
```
All day, all night, Marianne   Down by the seaside siftin sand
```
   C                  G7                         C
```
Even little children love Marianne Down by the seaside siftin sand

When she walks along the shore people pause to greet
White birds fly around her
Little fish come to her feet
In her heart is love but I'm the only mortal man
Who's allowed to kiss my Marianne
 Don't rush me CHORUS

When we marry we will have a time you never saw
I will be so happy I will kiss my mother in law
Children by the dozen and in our bamboo hut
One for every palm tree and cokynut
Hurry up now CHORUS

I WANNA GO HOME (also 97)

C
Sailed on the sloop John B My granddaddy and me
                          G7   C
'round nassau town we did roam We'd been drinkin' all night
              F
Well I got into a fight Yeah and I feel so broke up
G7   C
 I wanna go home

Hoist up the John B sail's See how the mainsail sets
Send for the captain ashore And let me go home
I wanna go home, I wanna go home, yeah
'cause I feel so broke up, I wanna go home
Yes I do
he's so broke up, lord, I wanna go home)

Well captain's a wicked man He gets drunk any time he can
And he don't give a damn for grandpappy No, nor me
He kicks us around And he knocks us about
Well I feel so broke up, I I wanna go home

Well pull up the John B's sails See how the mainsail sets
Send for the captain ashore And let me go home
I wanna go home Well, I wanna go home
'cause I feel so broke up I wanna go home
(yes I do)

I feel so broke up Lord, that I wanna go home

FAREWELL, ADELITA
(Bob Shane/Jack Splittard)

```
   C     G7         C
Adelita, 'tis time we remembered
        F                         G7
that only one hour more and I must go
                       F   C
To the hills of Sierra Del Prado
              G7     C
for the glory of our Mexico.
```

CHORUS
```
     G7                      C
Oh, Adelita, promise you'll remember
          G7                          C
the happy hours that now have long gone by.
                                  F
Oh, Adelita, we'll share these tender moments.
   G7                     C
Adelita, it hurts me when you cry.
```

Adelita, the time is here to leave you.
Once again, now, I'll kiss away your tears.
In my heart I will hold you forever
 and our love, it will live through the years.
CHORUS

KINGSTON TRIO

TOM DOOLEY

CHORUS
   E
Hang down your head Tom Dooley
                        B7
Hang down your head and cry
E
Hang down your head Tom Dooley
B7   *E*
Poor boy you're bound to die, Well now boy

I met her on the mountain
There I took her life
Met her on the mountain
Stabbed her with my knife, well now boy
CHORUS

This time tomorrow
Reckon where I'll be
Hadn't been for Grayson'
I'd be in Tennnesee, well now boy
CHORUS

This time tomorrow
Reckon where I'll be
Down in some lonesome valley
Hangin' from a tall oak tree, well now boy
CHORUS

THE M T A
Kingston Trio

G   C
Now let me tell you of the story of a man named Charlie
   G   D
On a tragic and fateful day.
   G   C
He put ten cents in his pocket, kissed his wife and family,
             D   G
And went to ride on the MTA.

CHORUS
G   C
Well did he ever return? No he never returned,
   G   D
And his fate is still unlearned.
   G   C
He may ride forever 'neath the streets of Boston,
   G   D   G
He's the man who never returned.

Charlie handed in his dime at the Kendell Square station,
And he changed for Jamaica Plain.
When he got there the conductor told him, "One more nickel."
Charlie couldn't get off that train.
CHORUS
Now all night long Charlie rides through the station
Crying, "What will become of me?
How can I afford to see my sister in Chelsea,
Or my cousin in Roxbury?"

GREENBACK DOLLAR
Kingston Trio

Em
Some people say I'm a no count
Others say I'm no good
but I'm just a natural born traveling man
D   Em
doin' what I think I should, oh yeah
D   Em
Doin' what I think I should

REFRAIN
           G   C   G   C
And I don't give a damn about a greenback dollar
G   C   G   C
Spend it fast as I can
G   C   G   C
But a wailing song a good guitar
        D   Em
The only thing that I understand, poor boy
        D   Em
The only thing that I understand

When I was a little baby
My Mama said hey son
Travel where you will and learn to be a man
and sing what must be sung, poor boy
Sing what must be sung
REFRAIN

REUBEN JAMES
Kingston Trio

C   G7   C
Have you heard of the ship called the good Rueben James?
           G7   C
Armed by hard-fighting men both of honor and of fame.
         F   C
She flew the Stars And Stripes of the land of the free.
          G7   C
But tonight she's in her grave at the bottom of the sea.
CHORUS
C   F
Tell me what were their names. Tell me what were their names.
 G7   C
Did you have a friend on the good Rueben James?
            F
Tell me what were their names. Tell me what were their names.
 G7   C
Did you have a friend on the good Rueben James?

One hundred men went down to their dark and watery grave.
When that good ship went down, only fourty-four were saved.
T'was the last day of October when they saved the fourty-four
From the dark, icey waters of that cold Iceland shore.
CHORUS
It was there in the dark on that cold and watery night.
That they watched for the U-boat, and they waited for a fight.

TIJUANA JAIL
Kingston Trio

```
G            C              G
We went one day, about a month ago
              D         G
To have a little fun, in Mexi-co
            C            G
We ended up at the gambling spot
                D                    G
Where the liquor flowed and the dice were hot
```

CHORUS:
```
            C              G
So here we are, in the Tijuana jail
            D          G
Ain't got no friends to go our bail
            C                  G
And here we'll stay cause we can't pay
            D              G
Just send our mail, to the Tijuana jail
```

I was throwing the dice, racking in the dough   (long green)
And then I heard the whistle blow
We started to run when a man in blue
Said "Senior come with me cause I want you."
CHORUS:

Just five hudnred dollars and they'll set us free
I couldn't raise a penny if it threathened me
I know five hundred don't sound like much   (cheap)
But just try to find somebody to touch
CHORUS:

A WORRIED MAN
The Kingston Trio)

CHORUS:

   C
It takes a worried man to sing a worried song
 F   C
It takes a worried man to sing a worried song
                        Am
It takes a worried man to sing a worried song
          Dm   G7   C
I'm worried now but I won't be worried long

                             C
Got myself a Cadillac thirty dollars down
F   C   C
Got myself a brand new house five miles out of town
                              Am
Got myself a gal named Sue treats me really fine
        Dm   G7   C
Yes, she's my baby and I love her all the time

CHORUS:

I've been away on a business trip travelin' all around
I got a gal and her name is Sue, prettiest gal in town
She sets my mind to worryin' every time I'm gone
I'll be home tonight so I won't be worried long

EVERGLADES
Kingston Trio

G
He was born and raised around Jacksonville.
   C   G
A nice young man, not the kind to kill.
     G   C
But a jealous fight and a flashing blade
D7   G
sent him on the run to the Everglades.
G   Dm7   G
Runnin' like a dog through the Everglades.

Now the possee went in and they came back out
They said he'll die and there ain't no doubt
It's an eye for an eye so the debt is paid
He won't last long in the Everglades
A man can't live in the Everglades

CHORUS:
G   C   Dm
Where a man can hide and never be found
    D   G
and have no fear of the bayin' hounds.
G   C
But he better keep movin' and don't stand still.
      D   G
 If the 'skeeters don't get 'em then the 'gaters will.

EL MATADOR
Kingston Trio

Aye, To-ro-ro, she is here, Aye, Matador.
I feel her eyes;
They are wide with excitement and fear.
I feel her heart
For it cries when the horns are too near,
I will be bold;
Brave and swift will I be,
And I will be nu-mer-o u-no.
To-re-ro fi-no.
She'll dream tonight of me.

(chorus)
O-le,o-le,o-le! Viva El Matador!
O-le,o-le,o-le! Viva El Matador!

Aye,To-ro-ro, she is here, Aye, Matador.
I see her smile And I see there the reason she came,
To-ro, come closer,
Come hear and I'll whisper her name.
You may be brave,
And as bold as you're black
But I will be nu-mber-o u-no,
To-re-ro fi-no,
To--ro, come back.

COPLAS REVISITED

```
Am            E      F              C
```
Chile verde me pedis te Chile verde te dare
```
              G      F         E
```
Vama nos para la huer ta con alla te lo cortare
Tell them what it means. The national safety council wishes me to inform you. Do not drink while driving (Porque) Youre' lible to hit a bump and spill the whole thing
```
Am            E      F              C
```
Di ce que los de fu ca sa Ninguno me puede ver
```
              G      F            E
```
Diles que no basta el agua que a cabo lahan de beber
Parlez vous Italiano? Tell your parents not to muddy the water around us (Forque) Our group has 25% fewer cavities clean water
```
Am            E      F                  C
```
La mula que yo mente la monto hoy mi compadre
```
              G      F              E
```
Eso a mil no me importa pues yo la mon te primero
Oi vey Hui. Show me a cowboy who rides side saddle and I will show you a gay ranchero, Now the bad verses Coplas!
```
E         Am      G            F            E
```
Hui Coplas Lai lai lai lai hum de lai lai la hum de lai lai lai
```
Am        G          F            E
```
Lai lai lai lai hum de lai lai la hum de lai lai lai
```
Am            E  F                    C
```
La noche que me case No pudde dormirmeun rato
```
              G      F             E
```
Por estar toda la noche corriendos detras de un gato
```
Am            E  F                   C
```
Me dejiste que fue un gato Que entro por tu balcon
```
              G       F             E
```
Yo no tisto gato prieto consombrero y panta

HI LILI LILI LO
(Fabares Shelly)

G   D
A song of love is a sad song, Hi-Lili, Lili, Lo

A song of love is a song of woe
                  G
Don't ask me how I know
G
A song of love is a sad song
                     D
For I have loved and it's so

                                                           D
I sit at the window and watch the rain, Hi-Lili, Lili, Lo
                                                        G
Tomorrow I'll probably love again, Hi-Lili, Lili, Lo.

Make your OWN VERSES....

G   D
I know a guy whose name is Ed, Hi-Lili, Lili, Lo
                                              G
He never gets his ass outa' bed, Hi-Lili, Lili, Lo
G   D
Hi-Lili, Lili, Lili, Hi-Lili, Lili Lo
                        D
Hi-Lili, Lili, Lili, Hi-Lili, Lili, Lo

RASPBERRIES, STRAWBERRIES
(Kingston Trio)

Intro: D D/E D/F# D/E D
SPEAK THIS A young man goes to Paris As every young man should. There's something in the air of France That does a young man good

 Amaj   D7   G   Am Am7
That does a young man good
REFRAIN
D7   G
La la la la la la la la la la la la la la la...
G   C   Am
Raspberries, strawberries, the good wines we brew
D7
Here's to the girls in the countryside
                     G
The ones we drink them to

The Paris nights are warm and fair, The summer winds are soft
A young man finds the face of love, In every field and loft, In every field and loft
In every field and loft
REFRAIN

 An old man returns to Paris, As every old man must
He finds the winter winds blow cold, His dreams have turned to dust
His dreams have turned to dust
His dreams have turned to dust
RETRAIN

Whom we must bid adieu

SINKING OF THE REUBEN JAMES
(Woodie Guthrie)

```
D                             G
What were their names, tell me what were their names?
A7                     D
Did you have a friend on the good Reuben James?


D                                       A7            D
Have you heard of a ship called that good Reuben James?
                                A7       D
Manned by hard-fighting men both of honor and fame
                        D7       G       D
She flew the Stars and Stripes of the Land of the Free
                        D       A7          D
But tonight she's in her grave at the bottom of the sea.
```

CHORUS
```
D                             G
```
What were their names, tell me what were their names?
```
   A7                  D
```
Did you have a friend on the good Reuben James?
```
                              G
```
Tell me, what were their names, what were their names?
```
   A7                        D
```
Did] you have a friend on the good Reuben James?

It was there in the dark of that uncertain night
That we waited for U-boats and waited for that fight
Then a whine and a rock and a great explosion roared
And they laid the Reuben James on that cold ocean floor.
CHORUS

Now, tonight there are lights in our country so bright
On the farms and the cities they're tellin' of that fight
And now our mighty battleships will sail the bounding main
And remember the men of the good Reuben James.
CHORUS

ROVING GAMBLER

```
  C    D7   C
```
I am a roving gambler I've gambled down in town
```
C                                           F    Am
```
Whenever I meet with a deck of cards, I lay my money down
```
 C          F           C     F C F C
```
Lay my money down, Lay my money down
```
  C         D7
```
I had not been in Washington many more weeks than three
```
                                       F      Am
```
'til I fell in love with a pretty little girl, She fell in love with me
```
 C          F          C     Am C
```
Fell in love with me, fell in love with me

She took me to her parlor she cooled me with a fan
She wispered low in her mama's ear
I love that gamblin' man I love that gamblin' man
Daughter oh dear daughter how can you treat me so
To leave your dear old mother and with a gambler go

I've gambled down in Washinton I've gambled down in Spain
I'm goin' down in Georgia
To gamble my last game To gamble my last game
Mother oh dear mother you know I love you well
But the love I have for the gamblin' man
No human tongue can tell

I hear the train a comin', a comin' round curve
A whistlin' and a blowin'
A strainin' every nerve A strainin' every nerve
Mother oh dear mother I'll tell you if I can
If you ever see me comin' back it will be with a gamblin' man
Be with a gamblin' man, be with a gamblin'man

THE ERIE CANAL

<pre>
A7   D   Gm   Dm   Gm   Dm
A7 Dm
</pre>
I've got a mule and her name is Sal. Fifteen miles on the Erie canal
<pre>
                        Gm   A
</pre>
She's a good o worker and a good ol' pal
<pre>
Dm   E7   Dm A7 Dm
</pre>
Fifteen miles on the Erie canal
<pre>
    F   Gm   A7
</pre>
We've hauled some barges in our day
<pre>
Dm   A
</pre>
Filled with lumber beer coal and hay
<pre>
    Dm   Gm   A
</pre>
And we know every inch of the way
<pre>
     Dm Gm Dm Bb7   Dm A7 Dm
</pre>
From Al...ba....ny to   Bu....ffa....lo
CHORUS
<pre>
C7 F   Bb
</pre>
Hey low bridge every body down
<pre>
F   Bbm   F   C7   F
</pre>
Low bridge for we're commin' to a town
<pre>
                  Bb   F   Bb
</pre>
An' you'll always know your neighbor You'll always know your pal
<pre>
     F   F7 Bb   Bbm   F C7 F
</pre>
If you've ever navigated on the Erie canal

BLOW YE WINDS

C
'Tis advertised in Boston, New York and Buffalo
  F   C   G7   C
A hundred hearty sailors a whalen' for to go

CHORUS
C
Blow ye winds o' mornin', Blow ye winds hi ho
F   C   G7
Haul away your runnin' gear and blow boys blow

They tell you of the clipper ships, A runnin' in and out
They say you'll take five hundred whales
Before you're six months out
CHORUS

The skipper's on the after deck a squintin' at the sails
When up above the look out spots a mighty school of whales
CHORUS

Then lower down the boats my boys and after him we'll travel
But if you ever get too near his tail, he'll kick you to the devil
CHORUS

And now that he is ours my boys We'll bring him along side
Then over with our blubber hooks and rob him of his hide
CHORUS

When we get home, our ship made fast
And we get through our sailin'
A brim'in glass around we'll pass and hang this blubber whalin'

I'D LIKE TO TEACH THE WORLD TO SING

CHORUS
    F
I'd like to build the world a home
       G7
and furnish it with love.
      C
Grow apple trees and honeybees
        Bb   C7
and snow-white turtle doves

    F   G7
I'd like to teach the world to sing in perfect harmony
  C   Bb   F
I'd like to hold it in my arms and keep it company
  F   G7
I'd like to see the world for once all standing hand in hand
     C
And hear them echo through the hills
 Bb   F
for peace throughout the land
             F   G7
That's the song I hear, let the world sing today
  C   Bb   F
A song of peace that echoes on and never goes away
                         G7
CHORUS

DRUNKEN SAILOR

Dm
What shall we do with the drunken sailor
C
What shall we do with the drunken sailor
Dm
What shall we do with the drunken sailor
     Am   Dm
Early in the morning

CHORUS
Dm
Yo, ho and up she rises
C
Yo, ho and up she rises
Dm
Yo, ho and up she rises
     Am   *Dm*
Early in the morning

Put him in the long boat til' he's sober
CHORUS
Pull out the plug and wet him all over
CHORUS
Heave him by the legs in a running bowline
CHORUS
Put him in the scuppers with the hose pipes on him
CHORUS
Shave him in the belly with a rusty razor
CHORUS

LEONARD COHEN

THE FUTURE
Leonard Cohen

Intro: Am

Am
Give me back my broken night
    Dm   G#dim   000101
My mirrored room, my secret life. Its Lonley here
            E7   Am
There's no one left to torture, give me absolute control
Dm   G#di   E7
Over every living soul. and lie beside me baby
          Am
That's an order!

CHORUS

 Dm   C
Things are going to slide (slide) in all directions
           Dm   C
Won't be nothing (won't be), nothing you can measure anymore
       Dm   F
The blizzard, the blizzard of the world
               F   Fm   133111
Has crossed the threshold, and it has overtrned
              C
The order of the soul
   G
When they said (they said) REPENT (repent), REPENT (repent)
     Am
I wonder what they meant, Repaeat three times

TAKE THIS WALTZ
Leonard Cohen

Intro: G   D

      G   Em
Now in Vienna there's ten pretty women
      G   G/F#   Em
There's a shoulder where Death comes to cry
      C   D
There's a lobby with nine hundred windows
      C   G G/F#   (F# 224311)
There's a tree where the doves go to die
        Em
There's a piece that was torn from the morning
     Am   Asus2/E   Am
And it hangs in the Gallery of Frost

C   G   G/F#
Ay, Ay, Ay, Ay
    Em
Take this waltz, take this waltz
          Am   C   D   A
With its "I'll never forget you, you know!"
   Em
This waltz, this waltz, this waltz, this waltz
     Am   Em
With its very own breath of brandy and Death
 Am   G   D
Dragging its tail in the sea

CLOSING TIME
Leonard Cohen

G
Ah, we're drinking and we're dancing, and the band is really happening
Em
and the Johnny Walker wisdom running high,
Bm
And my very sweet companion, she's the Angel of Compassion
Em
And she's rubbing half the world against her thigh.
C
And every drinker, every dancer, lifts a happy face to thank her
    G   B7   Em
And the fiddler fiddles something so sublime
     D
All the women tear their blouses off, the men they dance on the polka dots
    C
And it's partner found and it's partner lost and it's hell to pay when the fiddler stops
  G
It's Closing Time
   C
Yeah, the women tear their blouses off, the men they dance on the polka dots
     G   B7
And it's partner found and it's partner lost
    Em   C
and it's hell to pay when the fiddler stops
   G   D

it's Closing Time

C
I swear it happned just like this: a sigh, a cry, a hungry kiss
    G   B7
the Gates of Love they budged an inch
    Em   C
I can't say much has happened since, (can't say much has happened since, can't say much has happened since)
    G   D
but Closing Time, Closing Time
    Em
I loved you for your beauty, but that doesn't make a fool of me
Bm
you were in it for your beauty too
    Em
and I loved you for your body, there's a voice that sounds like God to me
    A   A7
Declaring (declaring) declaring (declaring)
    D
Declaring that you're body's really you (really really really really)

C
I loved you when our love was blessed, I love you now there's nothing left
    G   B7   Em
But sorrow and a sense of overtime
    D

And I miss you since the place got wrecked, but I just don't care what happens next
　C
Looks like freedom but it feels like death, it's something in between, I guess
　　　　G
it's Closing Time

　　　　C
Yeah. I miss you since the place got wrecked, by the winds of change and the weeds of sex
　G　　　　　　　　　　B7
Looks like freedom but it feels like death
　　　　Em　　　　　C
It's something in between, I guess
　　　　G　　　　　　D
It's Closing Time

EVERYBODY KNOWS
Leonard Cohen

Intro: Em   B   Em   Em

Em
Everybody knows that the dice are loaded
      C
Everybody rolls with their fingers crossed
      Em
Everybody knows the war is over
   C
Everybody knows the good guys lost
      Am   B
Everybody knows that the fight was fixed
         D   Em
The poor stay poor, the rich get rich
      F   B
That's how it goes
      Em
Everybody knows

CHORUS
          G   D
Everybody knows, everybody knows
     Em   D   C   G
That's how it goes, Everybody knows
     G   D
Everybody knows, everybody knows
      Em   D   C   G   Em
That's how it goes, everybody knows

OLD FAVORITES

JESSE JAMES

```
G            D7   G    C              G
```
Jesse James was a lad who killed many a man
```
                        D7
```
He robbed the Glendale train
```
     G    D7      G         C           G
```
He stole from the rich and he gave to the poor
```
                        D7   G
```
He'd a hand a heart and a brain
CHORUS
```
     C                Cm   G
```
Poor Jesse had a wife to morn for his life
```
                        D7
```
Three children they were brave
```
     G    D7    G         C         G
```
But that dirty little coward who shot Mr Howard
```
                  D7     G
```
Has laid poor Jesse in his grave

It was Robert Ford, that dirty little coward
I wonder how he does feel
For he ate of Jesse's bread and he slept in Jesse's bed
Then he gave poor Jesse a raw deal
CHORUS
Jesse was a man, a friend to the poor
He'd never see a man suffer pain
And with his brother Frank, he robbed the Chicago bank
And stopped the Glendale train
CHORUS
It was on a Saturday night when Jesse was at home
Talking with his family brave
Robert Ford came along like a thief in the night
And laid poor Jesse in his grave
CHORUS

LOGGER LOVE

```
   C                    G7                  C
As I sat down one evening inside a small café
                  F   A   G7           C
A forty year old waitress to me these words did say
                    G7                         C
I see that you are a logger and not just a common bum
                   F   A        G7          C
For no one but a logger stirs his coffee with his thumb
```

I had a logger lover, there are none like him today
If you poured whiskey on it, he would eat a bale of hay
He'd never shave his wiskers from off of his horney hide
He hammer in the bristles and bite them off inside

My lover came to see me on one freezing day
He held me in a fond embrace that broke three vertebrae
He kissed me when we parted, so hard that it broke my jaw
I could not speak to tell him, he forgot his mackinaw

The weather it tried to freeze him, it tried its level best
At forty degrees below zero he buttoned up his vest
It froze clear through to China, it froze to the stars above
At a hundred degrees below zero, it froze my logger love

And so I lost my lover and to this café I come
And here I wait for someone to stir coffee with his thumb

MRS. ROBINSON

CHORUS
*   G   Em*
And here's to you, Mrs. Robinson,
* G   Em   C   D7*
Jesus loves you more than you will know. Wo, wo, wo
*   G   Em*
God bless you, please, Mrs. Robinson,
G   Em   C   Am   E
Heaven holds a place for those who pray   Hey, hey, hey, hey, hey,

   E7
We'd like to know a little bit about you for our files.
       A7   A9
We'd like to help you learn to help yourself.
D7   G   C   Am
Look around you, all you see are sympathetic eyes.
E   D7
Stroll around the grounds until you feel at home.
CHORUS
 E7   A7
Hide it in a hiding place where no one ever goes
A7
Put it in your pantry with your cupcakes
D7   G   C   Am
It's a little secret just the Robinsons affair
E   D7
Most of all you've got to hide it from the kids

CHORUS

BIG BAD JOHN

REFRAIN
Gm C Gm C Gm C
    Am   F G   C Gm C
Big John, Big John, Big Bad John, Big John

Every morning at the mine you could see him arrive
He stood six-foot-six and weighed two-forty-five.
Kind of broad at the shoulder and narrow at the hip,
And everybody knew you didn't give no lip to Big John!
REFRAIN
Nobody seemed to know where John called home,
He just drifted into town and stayed all alone.
He didn't say much, a kinda quiet and shy,
And if he spoke at all, you just said, Hi to Big John!
Somebody said he came from New Orleans,
Where he got in a fight over a Cajun queen.
And a crashing blow from a huge right hand
Sent a Louisiana fellow to the promised land. Big John!
REFRAIN
Then came the day at the bottom of the mine
When a timber cracked and the men started crying.
Miners were praying and hearts beat fast,
And everybody thought that they'd breathed their last 'cept John.
Through the dust and the smoke of this man-made hell
Walked a giat of a man that miners knew well.
Grabbed a sagging timer and gave out with a groan,
And, like a giant oak tree, just stood there alone. Big John!
REFRAIN
And with all his strength, he gave a might shove;
Then a miner yelled out, "There's a light up above!"
And twenty men scrambled from a would-be grave,
And now there's only one left down there to save; Big John!
With jacks and timbers they started back down
Then came that rumble way down in the ground,
And smoke and gas belched out of that mine,
Everybody knew it was the end of the line for Big John!

I CAN SEE CLEARLY

D   G   D
I can see clearly now the rain has gone
            G   A
I can see all obstacles in my way
D   G   D
Gone are the dark clouds that had me blind
D   C   G   D
It's going to be a bright bright, bright sunshiny day
D   C   G   D
It's going to be a bright bright, bright sunshiny day

I can see clearly now the rain has gone
All of the bad feelings have disappeared
Here is the rainbow I've waiting fro
D   C   G   D
It's going to be a bright bright, bright sunshiny day
D   C   G   D
It's going to be a bright bright, bright sunshiny day

ENGLAND SWINGS

D   A7
Engeland swings like a pendulum do, Bobbies on bicycles two by two
D   G7
Westminster Abbey, the tower of Big Ben,
        D   A7   D
the rosy red cheeks of the little children
D   G   D
Now if you huff and puff and you finally save enough money up to take your family
A7   D   G
On a trip across the sea, take a tip before you take your trip
                    D
Let me tell you where to go, go to Engeland, Oh
D   A7
Engeland swings like a pendulum do, Bobbies on bicycles two by two
D   G7   D
Westminster Abbey, the tower of Big Ben, the rosy red cheeks of
A7   D
the little children
D   G
Mama's old pajamas and your papa's mustache,
D   A7
Fallin' out the window sill frolic on the grass
D   G
Tryin' to mock the way they talk but it's all in vain
D   G   D
Gappin' at the dapper men with derby hats and canes.

Engeland swings like a pendulum do, Bobbies on bicycles two by two
Westminster Abbey, the tower of Big Ben, the rosy red cheeks of the little children

RUNNING BEAR

        G   C   G
On the brink of the river stood Running Bear, young Indian brave.
                                       A7   D7
On the other side of the river stood his lovely Indian maid.
    G   C   G
Little White Dove was-a her name, such a lovely sight to see.
                                  D7   G
But their tribes fought each other, So their love could never be.

CHORUS
     C   G   D7   G
Running Bear loved little white Dove with a love big as the sky.
     C   G   D7   G
Running Bear loved little White Dove with a love that couldn't die.

He couldn't swim the raging river, cause the river was too wide.
He couldn't reach little White Dove, waiting on the other side.
In the moonlight he could see her, throwing kisses cross the waves.
Her little heart was beating faster, waiting there for her brave.
CHORUS

Running Bear dove in the water, Little White Dove did the same.
And they swam out to each other, through the swirling stream they came.
As their hands touched and their lips met, the raging river pulled them down.
No they'll always be together, in the Happy Hunting Ground.
CHORUS

SQUAWS ALONG THE YUKON

G   C
There's a salmon colored girl who sets my heart a whirl
   D7   G
Who lives along the Yukon far away
                                            C
With the northern lights a shine she rubs her nose to mine
   D7   G
She cuddles close and I can hear her say

CHORUS
G   C
Oo gah, oo gah muska, which means that I love you
*   D7   G*
If you will be my Baby, I'll oogah oogah muska you
*   C*
Then I take her hand in mine and set her on my knee
*   D7   G*
The squaws along the Yukon are good enough for me

She makes her underwear from hides of Grizzly bear
And bathes in ice cold water every day
Her skin I love to but I just can't touch it much
Because her fur lined parkas in the way
CHORUS

She has the air corp down, the sourdoughs hang around
Chechakos try to date her night and day
With landing gear that's fine and a fuselage divine
And a smile that you can see a mile away
CHORUS

WINGS OF A DOVE

              D   G
When troubles surround us, when evils come.
  Em   A7   D
The body grows weak; the spirit grows numb.
                  D   G
When these things beset us, he doesn't forget us.
              D   A7   D   G D
He sends down his love, on the wings of a dove.

CHORUS

            D   G
On the wings of a snow white dove, he sends his pure sweet love.
    D   A7   D
A sign from above, on the wings of a dove.

When Noah had drifted, on the flood many days
He searched for land, in various ways.
Troubles he had some, but wasn't forgotten
He sent him his love, on the wings of a dove.
CHORUS

When Jesus went down, to the waters that day
He was baptized, in the usual way
When it was done, God blessed his son.
He sent him his love, on the wings of a dove.
CHORUS

FROGGIE WENT A COURTING

     G
Mister Froggie went a courting and he did ride mm mmm
     G   D
Mister Froggie went a courting and he did ride mm mmm
     G
Mister Froggie went a courting and he did ride
    C   G   D   GF
A sword and a pistol by his side mmm mmm mmm

He went down to missy mousys door mm mmm
He went down to missy mousys door mm mmm
He went down to missy mousys door,
Where he had been many times gefore mmm mmm mmmm

Missy mousy are you within mmm mmm
Missy mousy are you within mmm mmm
Missy mousy are you within,
Yes kind sir I sit and spin mmm mmmm, mmm

He took missy mouse upon his knee mmm mmmm
He took missy mouse upon his knee mmm mmmm
He took missy mouse upon his knee
Said missy mouse will you marry me mmm mmm, mmm

BOTTLE OF WINE

CHORUS
C
Bottle of wine, fruit of the vine
                      G C
When you gonna let me get sober
C
Leave me alone, Let me go home
                  G C
Let me go back and start over

C   G   F   C
Ramblin round this dirty old town
      G   C
Singin for nickels and dimes
      G
Times getting rough
  F   C   G   C
I ain't got enough to get a little bottle of wine

Pain in my head, bugs in my bed
Pants are so old that they shine
Out on the street, tell the people I meet
Buy me a bottle of wine
CHORUS

Preacher will preach, teacher will teach
Miner will dig in the mine
I ride the rods, trusting in God
Huggin' my bottle of wine
CHORUS

FRANKIE AND JOHNNY

C
Frankie and Johnny were lovers, Oh, Lordy how they could love.
F   C
They swore to be true to each other, true as the stars above.
        G7   C
He was her man, but he done her wrong. So wrong.

Frankie and Johnny went walking, Johnny in his brand new suit.
Oh good Lord says Frankie, don't my Johnny look cute.
He was her man, but he done her wrong, so wrong.

Johnny said I've got to leave you, but I won't be very long
Don't you wait up for me hone, nor worry while I'm gone.
He was her man, but he done her wrong.

Frankie went down to the corner, stopped in to buy her some beer.
Says to the fat bartender, has my Johnny man been here?
He was her man, but he done her wrong.

Well I ain't going to tell you no story, ain't going to tell you no lie.
Johnny went by, bout an hour ago, with a girl name Nellie Blye.
He was your man, but he's doin you wrong.

Frankie went home in a hurry; she didn't go there for fun.
She hurried home to get a hold, of Johnny's shooting gun.
He was her man, but he's doin her wrong

Frankie took a cab at the corner, says Driver, step on this can.
She was just a desperate women, getting' two-timed by her man.
He was her man, but he's doin her wrong

Frankie got out at South Clark street, looked in a window so high
Saw her Johnny man alovin' up, that high brown Nellie Blye.
He was her man, but he's doin her wrong

Johnny saw Frankie a comin', out the back door he did scoot.
But Frankie took aim with her pistol, and the gun went root-a-toot-toot.
He was her man, but he done her wrong.

The sheriff arrested poor Frankie, took her to jail that same day
He locker her up in dungeon cell, and threw the key away.
She shot her man, though he done her wrong.

JUST WALKING IN THE RAIN

                  C
Just walking in the rain, Getting soaking wet
Dm   G7   C   G7
Torturing my heart, By trying to forget

No chord   C
Just walking in the rain, So alone and blue
Dm   G7   C F C C7
All because my heart, Still remembers you

F
People come to windows
C   G7   C
They always stare at me
D7
Shake there heads in sorrow
      G7
Saying who can that fool be

No chord   C
Just walking in the rain, Thinking how we met
Dm   G7   C
Knowing things have changed, Somehow I can't forget

HEARTBREAK HOTEL

D7
Now since my baby left me I've found a new place to dwell
Down at the end of lonely street at Heartbreak Hotel
     G7   D
I'm so lonely I'm so lonely
     G7   D
I'm so lonely that I could die
D7
And though it's always crowded, You can still find some room, for broken hearted lovers To cry there in their gloom
     G7   D
And be do lonely, Oh so lonely
     G7   D
Oh so lonely they could die

The bellhops tears keep flowing, The desk clerk's dressed in black
They've been so long on lonely street, They never will go back
Oh, they're so lonely
They're so lonely they pray to die

So if your baby leaves you and you have a tale to tell
Just take a walk down lonely street to Heartbreak Hotel
Where you'll be lonely, and I'll be lonely
We'll be so lonely that we could die

THE BATTLE OF NEW ORLEANS

   G   C
In eighteen and fourteen we took a little trip.
 D7   G
Along with Colonel Jackson down the mighty Mississip
                             C
We took a little bacon and we took a little beans
      D7   G
And we met the bloody British near the town of new Orleans.
CHORUS
  G

We fired our guns and British kept a comin'.
                            D7   G
There wuzn't nigh as many as they wuz a while a go.

We fired once more and they began a runnin'
                     D7   D
On down the Mississippi to the Gulf of Mexico.

We looked down the river and we seed the British come
There must have bee a hundred of em beaten on the drum
They stepped so high and they made their bugles ring
While we stood beside our cotton bales and didn't do a thing
CHORUS

Old Hickry said we'd take 'em by surprise
If we didn't fire a musket till we looked 'em in the eyes
We hold our fire till we seed their faces well
The we opened up our squirrel guns and really gave 'em hell.
CHORUS

WABASH CANNON BALL

  G   C
Oh listen to the jingle, the tumble and the roar
    D   G
Of the mighty rushing engine as she streams along the shore
  G   C
The mighty rushing engine, hear the bell and whistle call
D   G
As you roll along in safety, On the Wabash Cannon Ball

I stood on the Atlantic Ocean, The wide Pacific shore
To the queen of the flowing mountains,To the southbell by the door
She's long and tall and handsome, And loved by one and all
She's a modern combination, Called the Wabash Cannonball

CHORUS:
Oh listen to the jingle, The rumble and the roar
As she glides along the woodlands,
Through the hills and by the shores
Hear the mighty rush of engines, Hear the lonesome hobos' call
We're travelling through the jungles, On the Wabash Cannonball

The eastern states are dandies, So the western people say,
From New York to St. Louis, And Chicago by the way,
Through the hills of Minnesota, Where the rippling waters fall,
No chances can be taken, On the Wabash Cannonball
CHORUS

Here's to Daddy Klaxton, May his name forever stand
Will he be remembered, Through parts of all our land
His earthly race is over, And the curtain 'round him falls
We'll carry him on to victory, On the Wabash Cannonball
CHORUS

MICHAEL ROW THE BOAT ASHORE

CHORUS
D   G   D
Michael row the boat ashore hallleluyah
*   Em   A7   D*
Michael row the boat ashore hallleluyah

D   G   D
Michaels boat is a music boat halleluyah
                         Em   A7   D
Michaels boat is a music boat halleluyah

Sister help to trim the sail, halleluyah
Sister help to trim the sail, halleluyah

The river Jordan is chilly and cold, halleluyah
The river Jordan is chilly and cold, halleluyah

JACKSON

  C
We got married in a fever, hotter than a pepper sprout
  C
We've been talkin' 'bout Jackson ever since the fire went out
C7   F   F9   C
I goin' to Jackson.Goin' to mess around
   C7   F   G7   G   C
I'm goin' to Jackson You know I'm pleasure bound

Well, you my sweet daddy, go ahead and wreck your health
Play your hand like a lover man,
and make a big fool of yourself
Go on to Jackson, comb your hair
Gotta snowball Jackson, see if I care

When I breeze in to that city, people gonna scrape and bow
All them women gonna beg me
to Teach 'm what they don't know how
I'm going to Jackson, turn loose my code
I'm goin' to Jackson Goodbye that's all she wrote

When they laugh at you in Jackson, I'll be dancin' on the pony keg
Then I'll lead you 'round town like a scolded hound
with your tail tucked between your legs
So go on down to Jackson, you big talkin' man
I'll be waitin' in Jackson, behind my Japan fan

COOL WATER

```
    E           B7              E              B7
All day I faced the barren waste without the taste of water
    E
Cool water
A              B7              E       A      E
Old Dan and I with throats burnt dry and souls that cry for
water
B7         E
Cool clear water
                        B7
Keep a movin' Dan don't you listen to him Dan
        E
He's a devil not a man
        B7                      E
And he spreads the burning sand with water
A              E                        A
Dan can you see that big green tree where the water's
running free
        B7                  E
And it's waiting there for you and me
```

The nights are cool and I'm a fool
Each star's a pool of water, cool water
But with the dawn I'll wake and yawn
And carry on to water, cool, clear water

The shadows sway and seem to say
Tonight we pray for water, cool water
And wa up there he'll hear our prayer
And show us where there's water, cool clear water

CRY OF THE WILD GOOSE

Am Dm
Tonight I heard the wild goose cry
                     E7
Wingin' north in the lonely sky
Am Dm
Tried to sleep but it warn't no use
                            Am
'Cause I am a brother to the old wild goose
Am Dm
My heart knows where the wild goose goes
                       E7
And I must go where the wild goose goes
Am
Wild goose brother goose which is best
     Dm   E7   Am
A wanderin' or a heart at rest?

THE REVEREND MR. BLACK

SPEAK THIS He rode easy in the saddle, he was tall and lean And at first you'd a thought noting but a streak of mean Could make a man so downright strong
But one look in his eyes and you knowed you was wrong
He was a mountain man and I want you to know he could preach hot hell or freezen' snow. He carried a bible in a canvas sack, and folks just called him the reverend Mr Black. He was poor as a begger but rode like a king. Sometimes in the evenin' I could hear him sing...
CHORUS

```
C                F         C              G7        C
```
I got to walk that lonesome valley, I got to walk it by myself
```
   C7      F         C              G7      C
```
Oh nobody else can walk it for me, I got to walk it by myself

If ever I could have thought this man in black was soft and had any yellow in his back, I gave that notion up to the day that a lumberjack came in and it wasn't to pray. He kicked open the meeting house door, and he cussed everybody up and down the floor. Then when things got quiet in the place he walked up and cussed in the preacher's face. He hit the reverend like a kick of a mule and to my way of thinkin' it took a pure fool to turn the other cheek to that lumberjack but that's what he did, the reverend Mr Black. He stood like a rock, a man among men, and let that lumberjack hit him again. And then with a voice as kind as could be, he cut him down like a big oak tre, when he said...
CHORUS
It's been many a year since we dad to part, and I guess I learned his ways by heart. Yes, I can still hear sermons ring down in the valley where he used to sing. I followed him, yes sir, and I don't regret it and I hope that I'll always be a credit to his memory 'Cause I want you to understand, the Reverend Mr Black was my old man

HAKUNA MATATA

INTRO & CHORUS
```
     F    Bb/F                  C
```
Hakuna matata   what a wonderful phrase
```
C/E     F     D/F#             G7
```
Hakuna Matata, ain't no passin' craze
```
  E/G#     Am    C/E     F          D/F#
```
It means no worries for the rest of your days
```
       C/G          G
```
It's our problem free philosophy
```
         C
```
Hakuna matata Hakuna matata

C Dm   C G Dm   Am   G

Yeah. It's our motto!What's a motto?Nothing. What's a-motto with you?Those two words will solve all your problemsThat's right. Take Pumbaa here
```
            Bb          F          C
```
Why, when he was a young warthog...
```
     Bb      F         C
```
When I was a young wart hog

Very nice…. Thanks
```
   Eb                      F
```
He found his aroma lacked a certain appeal
```
C                             G
```
He could clear the savannah after every meal
```
     Bb          F/A    F       C
```
I'm a sensitive soul though I seem thick-skinned
```
       E                              G
```
And it hurt that my friends never stood downwind

HAKUNA MATATA

   G7sus C   F/C C
And oh, the shame, **He was a shamed**
                       G
Thought of changin' my name
      C/G G
Oh, What's in a name?
        F/A   Bb
And I got downhearted
     Eb/Bb Bb
How did ya feel?   Every time that I...

Hey! Pumbaa! Not in front of the kids!
Oh. Sorry

CHORUS
Hakuna Matata! What a wonderful phrase
Hakuna Matata! Ain't no passing craze
It means no worries for the rest of your days
It's our problem-free philosophy Hakuna Matata!

C   Dm   C   G   Dm   Am   G
 C   F/C   G/B
Hakuna Matata! Hakuna matata!
 G/B   F/A
Hakuna Matata! Hakuna matata!
 C/G   G
Hakuna Matata! Hakuna matata! Hakuna Matata!
Hakuna—
    E/G   Am   C/E   F   D/F#
It means no worries for the rest of your days
      C/G   G7   E/G#   Am
It's our problem-free philosophy Hakuna Matata!
(Repeats)
I say "Hakuna" I say "Matata"

THE HAPPY WANDERER

C   G7
I love to go a wandering, Along the mountain track
            C   F   G7   C
And as I go I love to sing, My Knap sack on my back

CHORUS
      G7   C
Val de ri Val de ra
      G7   C   *G7   C*
Val de ra Val de ha ha ha ha ha ha Val de ri Val de ra
    F   G7   C
My knap sack on my back

I love to wander by the stream, That dances in the sun
So joyously it calls to me,
Come join my happy song
CHORUS Come join my happy song

I wave my hat to all I meet, And they wave back to me
And blackbirds call so loud and sweet,
From every greenwood tree
CHORUS From every Greenwood tree

High over head the skylark wing, They never rest at home
But just like me they love to sing,
As over the world we roam
CHORUS As over the world we roam

Oh may I go a wandering, Until the day I die
Oh may I always laugh and sing,
Beneath God's clear blue sky
CHORUS Beneath God's clear blue sky

IF I WERE A RICH MAN

CHORUS
D
If I were a rich man,
  D
Ya ha deedle deedle, bubba bubba deedle deedle dum.
A7   *Dm*
All day long I'd biddy biddy bum.
 G#dim   *A7*   *D*
If I were a wealthy man. I wouldn't have to work hard.
 A
Ya ha deedle deedle, bubba bubba deedle deedle dum.
A7   *Dm*   *E7*   *A7*   *D*
If I were a biddy biddy rich, Yidle-diddle-didle-didle man.

 D   Gm   Gm7   C7
I'd build a big tall house with rooms by the dozen,
 F   Fbmaj7   Cm6
Right in the middle of the town.
D7   Gm   A7   D
A fine tin roof with real wooden floors below.
D7   Gm   Fm7   C7
There would be one long staircase just going up,
    F   F7   C
And one even longer coming down,
 D7 Gm   Gdim   A
And one more leading nowhere, just for show.
  D7   G   G7   A7   D
I'd fill my yard with chicks and turkeys and geese and ducks
    F6   B7
For the town to see and hear.
 D7   Gm   Gm7   C7
And each loud "cheep" and "swaqwk" and "honk" and "quack"
    F   F7   C6   D7
Would land like a trumpet on the ear,

IF I WERE A RICH MAN

        Gm   G#dim   C
As if to say "Here lives a wealthy man."
CHORUS

I see my wife, my Golde, looking like a rich man's wife
With a proper double-chin.
Supervising meals to her heart's delight.
I see her putting on airs and strutting like a peacock.
Oy, what a happy mood she's in.
Screaming at the servants, day and night.

The most important men in town would come to fawn on me!
They would ask me to advise them,
Like a Solomon the Wise.
"If you please, Reb Tevye..."
"Pardon me, Reb Tevye..."
Posing problems that would cross a rabbi's eyes!
And it won't make one bit of difference if i answer right or wrong.
When you're rich, they think you really know!

If I were rich, I'd have the time that I lack
To sit in the synagogue and pray.
And maybe have a seat by the Eastern wall.
And I'd discuss the holy books with the learned men,
several hours every day.
That would be the sweetest thing of all.

CHORUS.

. VAYA CODIOS

```
C                        Am       G7
Now the hacienda's dark the town is sleeping
        F              G7    C       C7
Now the time has come to part the time for weeping
F                C   G7      F  G7  C
Va ya con dios my darling, Vay ya con dios my love
```

Now the village mission bells are softly ringing
If you listen with your heart You'll hear them singing
Va ya con dios my darling, Vay ya con dios my love

Wherever you may be I'll be beside you
Although you're many million dreams away
Each night I'll say a prayer to guide you
To hasten every lonely hour of every lonely day
Now the dawn is breaking through a gray tomorrow
But the memories we share are there to borrow
Va ya con dios my darling, Vay ya con dios my love

OH MY DARLING CLEMINTINE

G   D7
In a cavern, in a canyon excavating for a mine
                     G   D7   G
Dwelt a miner fourty niner And his daughter Clemintine

CHORUS
  G   D7
Oh, my Darling, Oh my Darling, Oh my darling Clemintine
                          G   D7   G
You are lost and gone forever, Dreadful sorry, Clemintine

Light she was and like a fairy
And her shoes were number nine
Herring boxes without topses
Sandals were for Clemintine
CHORUS

Drove her ducklings to the water
Every morning just at nine
Hit her foot against a splinter
Fell into the foaming brine
CHORUS

Ruby lips above the water
Blowing bubbles soft and fine
Las for me I was no swimmer
So I lost my Clemintine
CHORUS

GRANDFATHER'S CLOCK

G　　　　　D7　　　　G　　　　　C
My grandfathers clock was too large for the shelf
　G　　　　　D7　　　G
So it stood ninety years on the floor
　　　　　　　　　　　　　C　　　　G
It was taller by half than the old man himself
　　G　　　　　　　　D7　　　　G
Though it weighed not a pennyweight more
　　　　　　　　　　　　　　　C　　　　G
It was bought on the morn of the day he was born
　　　　　　　　　D7
And was always his treasure and pride

CHORUS
　　　G　　D　　G　　　　C
But it stopped short, never to go again,
　　　G　D7　　G
When the old man died

Ninety years without slumbering Tick Tock tick tock
His life seconds numbering tick tock tick tock
　　　　　　　D　　G　　　　C
It stopped short, never to go again
　　　G　D7　G
When the old man died

In watching its pendulum swing to and fro
Many hours he spent while a boy
And his childhood and manhood the clock seemed to know
And to share both his grief and his joy
For it struck twenty four when he entered the door
With a blooming and beautiful bride
CHORUS

WHEN THE SAINTS GO MARCHING IN

CHORUS
C
Oh when the saints go marchin in
                        G7
Oh when the saints go marchin in
    C   *F*
Lord I want to be in that number
        C   *G7*   *CF*
When the saints go marching in

C   F   G7
We are trav'ling in the footsteps, Of those who've gone before
     C   F   C   G7   C
But we'll all be reunited, On a new and sunlit shore
CHORUS
O when the Saints go marching in, When the Saints go marching in
O Lord I want to be in that number, When the Saints go marching in
CHORUS
And when the sun refuse to shine, And when the sun refuse to shine
O Lord I want to be in that number, When the Saints go marching in
CHORUS
When the moon turns red with blood, When the moon turns red with blood
O Lord I want to be in that number, When the Saints go marching in
CHORUS
On that hallelujah day, On that hallelujah day
O Lord I want to be in that number, When the Saints go marching in
CHORUS

LEMON TREE
(Peter, Paul, Mary)

```
     D    A7   D                      A7    D
When I was just a lad of ten, my father said to me,
                 A7   D                 A7      D
"Come here and take a lesson from the lovely lemon tree."
     G      D7    G                        D7   G
"Don't put your faith in love, my boy", my father said to me,
          D7       G                 D7       G
"I fear you'll find that love is like the lovely lemon tree."
```

CHORUS
```
     D                                         A7
```
Lemon tree very pretty and the lemon flower is sweet
```
                                               D
```
but the fruit of the poor lemon is impossible to eat.
```
     D                                         A7
```
Lemon tree very pretty and the lemon flower is sweet
```
                                               D
```
but the fruit of the poor lemon is impossible to eat.

One day beneath the lemon tree, my love and I did lie
A girl so sweet that when she smiled the stars rose in the sky.
We passed that summer lost in love beneath the lemon tree
the music of her laughter hid my father's words from me:
CHORUS

One day she left without a word. She took away the sun.
And in the dark she left behind, I knew what she had done.
She'd left me for another, it's a common tale but true.
A sadder man but wiser now I sing these words to you:
CHORUS

THIS LAND IS YOUR LAND

CHORUS
G   C   G
This land is your land, this land is my land,
* D   G*
From California, to the New York Island,
*   C   G*
From the Redwood Forest, to the Gulf Stream Waters,
* D   G*
This land was made for you and me.

I roamed and rambled, and I followed my footsteps
To the sparkling sands of her diamond deserts
And all around me a voice was singing
This land was made for you and me!
CHORUS

As I went walking that ribbon of highway
I saw above me that endless skyway
I saw below me those golden valleys
This land was made for you and me!
CHORUS

As the sun was shining, and I was strolling,
And the wheat fields waving, and the dust clouds rolling,
As the fog was lifting, a voice was saying
"This land was made for you and me!"
CHORUS

ARE YOU LONESOME TONIGHT

        C   Em   Am
Are you lonesome tonight, do you miss me tonight?
    C   C7   F
Are you sorry we drifted apart?
       G   G7
Does your memory stray to a brighter sunny day
                                C
When I kissed you and called you sweetheart?
   C7   F
Do the chairs in your parlor seem empty and bare?
  D   rem   G
Do you gaze at your doorstep and picture me there?
  C   Em   D
Is your heart filled with pain, shall I come back again?
  rem   G7   C
Tell me dear, are you lonesome tonight?

I wonder if you're lonesome tonight
You know someone said that the world's a stage
And each must play a part.
Fate had me playing in love you as my sweet heart.
Act one was when we met, I loved you at first glance
You read your line so cleverly and never missed a cue
Then came act two, you seemed to change and you acted strange. And why I'll never know.

WALTZING MATILDA
(A. Patterson)

```
C                 G7      C
Once a jolly swagman , camped in a  billabong..
                                  G7
under the shade of a coolabahs Tree...
         C             G7         C              C
And he sang as he watched and waited till his billy boiled...
                         G7      C
Who'll come a waltzing Matilda with me-...
```

CHORUS
```
C                        F
```
Waltzing Matilda, Waltzing Matilda,.
```
 C                               G7
```
you'll come a waltzing Matilda with me
```
      C         G7          C
```
And she sang as watched and waited near the Billabong...
```
                   G7     C
```
you'll come a waltzing Matilda with me ...
```
                   G7     C
```
"Who'11 come a-waltzing Matilda with me?"

Down come a jumbuck to drink at the water hole
Up jumped a swagman and grabbed him in glee
And he sang as he stowed him away in his tucker bag
"You'll come a-waltzing Matilda with me'".
CHORUS
Up rode the Squatter a riding his thoroughbred
Up rode the Trooper- one, two, three
"Where's thst jumbuck you've got in your tucker bag?",
"You'11 come a-waltzing Matiltda with me".
CHORUS

STEWBALL

    D   Em
Oh stewball was a racehorse, and I wish he were mine.
            A   D   G A7 D
He never drank water, he always drank wine.

His bridle was silver, his mane it was gold.
And the worth of his saddle has never been told.

Oh the fairgrounds were crowded, and stewball was there
But the betting was heavy on the bay and the mare.

And a-way up yonder, ahead of them all,
Came a-prancin' and a-dancin' my noble stewball.

I bet on the grey mare, I bet on the bay
If I'd have bet on ol' stewball, I'd be a free man today.

Oh the hoot owl, she hollers, and the turtle dove moans.
I'm a poor boy in trouble, I'm a long way from home.

Oh stewball was a racehorse, and I wish he were mine.
He never drank water, he always drank wine.

WALK RIGHT IN
(Janis Joplin)

```
 C                       A   D7            G       C
Walk right in, sit right down, Daddy, let your mind roll on
 C                       A   D7
Walk right in, sit right down Daddy, let your mind roll on
 C
Everybody's talkin' 'bout a new way of walkin'
 D
Do you want to lose your mind?
 C                       A   D7            G       C
Walk right in, sit right down Daddy, let your mind roll on
```

Walk right in, sit right down Baby, let your hair hang down
Walk right in, sit right down Baby, let your hair hang down
Everybody's talkin' 'bout a new way of walkin'
Do you want to lose your mind?
Walk right in, sit right down Baby, let your hair hang down

[guitar interlude

Walk right in, sit right down Daddy, let your mind roll on
Walk right in, sit right down Daddy, let your mind roll on
Everybody's talkin' 'bout a new way of walkin'
Do you want to lose your mind?
Walk right in, sit right down Daddy, let your mind roll on
Daddy, let your mind roll on

NORTH TO ALASKA
(J. Horton)

CHORUS
C
Way up north, Way up north,
C   G7   Dm7 G7   C
North to Alaska, They're goin' North, the rush is on.
C   G7   Dm7 G7   C
North to Alaska, They're goin' North, the rush is on.

```
       C                   G7      Dm7  C     F   C
```
Big Sam left Seattle in the year of ninety two,
```
 C7    F                              C  F    C
```
With George Pratt, his partner, and brother, Billy, too.
```
 C7    F                              C  F    C
```
They crossed the Yukon River and found the bonanza gold.
```
              F       C        G7      Dm G7    C
F  C
```
Below that old white mountain just a little south-east of Nome.

Sam crossed the majestic mountains to the valleys far below.
He talked to his team of huskies
as he mushed on through the snow.
With the northern lights a-running wild
in the land of the midnight sun,
Yes, Sam McCord was a mighty man in the year of nineteen-one.

```
        C       G7 C       F
```
Where the river is winding, Big nuggets they're finding.
CHORUS

135. DELTA DAWN
(Alex Harvey)

CHORUS
A   D   A
Delta Dawn, what's that flower you have on?
*   E*
Could it be a faded rose from days gone by?
* A   D   A*
And did I hear you say he was a-meetin' you here today
* A   E   D   A*
To take you to his mansion in the sky-eye?

   A   G   A
She's forty-one and her daddy still calls 'er "baby"
                    G   A
All the folks 'round Brownsville say she's crazy
          D
'cause she walks downtown with her suitcase in her hand
              G   A
Lookin' for a mysterious dark-haired man
CHORUS

In her younger days they called her Delta Dawn
Prettiest woman you ever laid eyes on
Then a man of low degree stood by her side
Promised her he'd take her for his bride
CHORUS

MARGARITAVILLE
(Jimmy Buffet)

```
 D                          C
Nibblin' on sponge cake, Watchin' the sun bake
 A                                G
All of those tourists covered with oil Strummin' my six-
string
```

On my front porch swing
```
 D                        D7           C
Smell those shrimp they're beginnin' to boil
```

CHORUS:
```
G     A    D        D7
```
Wastin' away again in margaritaville
```
 G    A    D        D7
```
Searching for my lost shaker of salt
```
G     A    D              A      G
```
Some people claim that there's a woman to blame
```
   A   G        D
```
But I know it's nobody's fault

I don't know the reason I stayed here all season
Nothin' to show but this brand new tattoo
But it's a real beauty A mexican cutie
How it got here I haven't a clue

CHORUS Plus: **Now I think Hell, it could be my fault**

WATERMELLON MINE
(Tom Hall)

      G   C   Am
I was sitting in Miami pouring blended whisky down
         C   G   D   G
when this old grey black gentleman was cleaning up the lounge
    G   C   Am
there wasn't anyone around but this old man and me
    D   C   D G
the guy who tended bar was watching ironsides on TV
  G   C   Am
Uninvited, he sat down and opened up his mind
   C   G   D   G
On old dogs and children, and watermellon wine.

Have you ever had a drink of watermellon wine he asked
He told me all about it though i didn't answer back
Ain't but three things in life that's worth a solitary dime
That's old dogs and children, and watermellon wine.

He said women think about themselves
when their menfolk aren't around
And friends are hard to find when they discover that you're down
He said i tried it all when i was young and in my natural prime
Now it's old dogs and children and watermellon wine.

He said old dogs care about you even when you make mistakes
God bless little children while they're still too young to hate
 as he moved away I got my pen and copied down that line
On old dogs and children and watermellon wine.

I had to catch a plane up to atlanta the next day
As I left for my room i saw him picking up my change
That night I dreamed in peacefull sleep of shady summer times
 of old dogs and children and watermellon wine, Watermelon wine

SNEAKY SNAKE
(Tom Hall)

```
G                    G7       C            G
Boys and girls take] warning, If you go near the  lake
C              G       A7            D7
keep your eyes wide open And look for Sneaky Snake
     G               G7       C              G
Now maybe you won't see him And maybe you won't hear
    C            G         D7                    G
But he'll sneak up behind you And  drink all of your Root
Beer.
```

CHORUS:
```
         G                  C
And then Sneaky Snake goes dancin'
G         C        G
wigglin' and a-hissin' Sneaky Snake goes dancin'
A7         D7       G           G7
A gigglin' and a kissin' I dont like old Sneaky Snake,
   C                      G
He laughs too much, you see
    C                 G
When he goes wiggin' thru the grass
  D7                G
It tickles his under-neath.
```

Well, Sneaky Snake drinks Root Beer and he just makes me sick
When he is not dancin', he looks just like a stick
Now he doesn't have any arms or legs, you cannot see his ears
And while we are not lookin', he's stealin' all of our beer.
CHORUS
Sneaky Snake

I LIKE BEER (Tom Hall)

```
   G                        C        G
In some of my songs I have casually mentioned
G                     D
The fact that I like to drink beer
   G                   C       G
But this little song is more to the point
     D
so roll out the barrel and lend me your ear
```

(CHORUS)
```
        C                          G
I like beer It makes me a jolly good fellow
        C      D
I like beer, It helps me unwind

 and sometime it makes me feel mellow
G                         C              G
Whiskeys too rough, Champaign costs too much
                          C
vodka puts my mouth in gear
                          G
This little refrain should help me explain
        D          G
as a matter of fact I like beer
```

My wife often frowns when we're out on the town
I'm wearing a suit and a tie
She's sipping vermouth and she thinks I'm uncouth
When I yell when the waiter walks by
(Chorus)

Last night I dreamed that I passed from the scene
and I went to a place so sublime
the water was clear and it tasted like beer
then they turned it all into wine (ahhhh)

THUNDER ROAD

C
Let me tell the story, I can tell it all
  G7   C
About the mountain boy who ran illegal alcohol

His daddy made the whiskey, son, he drove the load
 G7   C
When his engine roared, they called the highway Thunder Road.

Sometimes into Ashville, sometimes Memphis town
The revenoors chased him but they couldn't run him down
Each time they thought they had him, his engine would explode
He'd go by like they were standin' still on Thunder Road.

(CHORUS)
                F   C
And there was thunder, thunder over Thunder Road
 G7   C
Thunder was his engine, and white lightning was his load
              F   C
There was moonshine, moonshine to quench the Devil's thirst
    G7   C
The law they swore they'd get him, but the Devil got him first.

On the first of April, nineteen fifty-four
A Federal man sent word he'd better make his run no more
He said two hundred agents were coverin' the state
Whichever road he tried to take, they'd get him sure as fate.

Son, his Daddy told him, make this run your last
The tank is filled with hundred-proof, you're all tuned up and gassed
Now, don't take any chances, if you can't get through
I'd rather have you back again than all that mountain dew.
(CHORUS)

FAST FREIGHT

    Am
As I listen for the whistle, lie awake and wait.
Gm   A7   Dm
Wish that railroad didn't run so near,

'cause the rattle and the clatter of the ol' fast freight
A7   Dm
keeps a-makin' music in my ear.

CHORUS:
Dm
Go bum again, go bum again.
D   C   D   Dm
Hear the whistle blow, hear the whistle blow.

Clickety clack, clickety clack, the wheels are saying to the railroad track,
*   Gm*
Dm
Well if you go you can't come back, if you go you can't come back,
well if you go you can't come back, if you go you can't come back,
If you go you can't come back..."

Well I wouldn't give a nickle for the man I used to be.
Worked as hard as any man in town. I got a pretty gal,
she thinks the world of me.
Man would be a fool to let her down...
CHORUS

So everynight I listen, wonder if it's late.
In my dreams I'm riding on that train. I feel pulse a-beatin',
with that ol' fast frieght,
and thank the lord I'm just a bum again.

RAINDROPS KEEP FALLING ON MY HEAD (Bacharach)

INTRO: F-C-Bb-C

F   Fmaj7
Raindrops keep falling on my head
 F7   Bb   Am
and just like the guy whose feet are too big for his bed,
D7   Am
nothing seems to fit,
  D7 Gm7
Those raindrops are fallin' on my head they keep fallin'
C7   F   Fmaj7
So I just did me some talkin' to the sun,
 F7   Bb   Am
and I said I didn't like the way he got things done
D7   Am
Sleepin' on the job,
  D7 Gm7
Those raindrops are fallin' on my head they keep fallin'
C7   F Fmaj7
But there's one thing I know,
  Bb   C   Am
the blues they send to meet me, won't defeat me
        D7   Gm7   Bb C Bb C
It won't be long till happiness steps up to greet me
 F   Fmaj7
Raindrops keep fallin' on my head,
  F7   Bb   Am
but that doesn't mean my eyes will soon be turnin' red,
D7   Am D7 Gm7
Cryin's not for me, cause I'm never gonna stop the rain by complainin'
C7   F C7
because I'm free, nothings worryin' me

MELLOW YELLOW
(Donovan)

```
D            G         D              A7 A Ab
I m just mad about Saffron, ....
G                    G7     A
I m just mad about Saffron, ....
     A7          D    G    A7     D   G
They call me Mellow Yellow, they ....
     A7         D   G A7
They call me Mellow ...

D                    G    D           A7 A Ab
I m just mad about Fourteen, ...
G                    G7    A
I m just mad about Fourteen, ...
    A7           D    G    A7     D   G
They call me Mellow Yellow, ...
    A7          D    G A7
They call me Mellow ....
```

Born high forever to fly, ...
Born high forever to fly, if you want ...
They call me Mellow Yellow, ...
They call me ...

Electrical banana, is going to ...
Electrical banana is ....
They call me Mellow Yellow ...
They call me ...

I m just mad about Saffron, ...
I m just mad about Saffron, ...
They call me Mellow Yellow, ...
They call me ....

HIGH HOPES
Writer(s): Cahn/Van Heusen

```
Calt                          Gdim      (Gdim 342300)
```
Next time you're found, with your chin on the ground,
```
       Dm7             G7   G6   G/B   C   (Dm7
000213)
```
There a lot to be learned, so look a - round. (G6
320000)

```
  C        Am7        Dm7       F       (Am7 002010)
```
Just what makes that little old ant
```
 Dm7       G7         C6          C     (C6 032210)
```
Think he'll move that rubber tree plant? (Cdim 231200)
```
  C        C7        F  Cdim   G7     G6    G/B   C
```
Anyone knows an ant can't move a rubber tree plant,
```
         C7        F          Cdim       C
```
But he's got high hopes, he's got high hopes,
```
Am7       D7   Am7    D7  Am7     G
```
He's got high apple pie, in the sky hopes.
```
  Am7 G/B C                 C7
```
So an - y time your gettin' low, 'stead of lettin' go,
```
 F       Dm7         Cdim
```
Just remember that ant --
```
G          D7   Dm7       G7         C
```
Oops there goes another rubber tree plant.

When troubles call, and your back's to the wall,
There a lot to be learned, that wall could fall.

Once there was a silly old ram
Thought he'd punch a hole in a dam;

No one could make that ram scram -- he kept buttin' that dam,
'Cause he had high hopes, he had high hopes,
He had high apple pie, in the sky hopes.
So an - y time your feelin' bad,'stead of feelin' sad,
Just remember that ram --
Oops there goes a billion kilowatt dam.

(Instrumental Interlude - First Five Lines of Verse)

    Am7   G/B C
All prob - lems just a toy balloon;
 C7   F   Dm7   Cdim
They'll be bursted soon -- they're just bound to go pop.
G   D7   Dm7   G7
Oops there goes another problem ker -
G   D7   Dm7   G7
Oops there goes another problem ker -
G   D7   Dm7   G7   C   G   C
Oops there goes another problem ker - plop, ker - plop?

DONOVAN

JENNIFER JUNIPER
Donovan

```
G        D      G       D      A7
Jen -    i-fer  Jun  -  i-per  lives upon the hill
G        D      G       D      A7
Jen -    i-fer Jun -    i-.per sitting very still...
D                       A7
Is she sleeping?  I don't think so.
D                       A7
Is she breathing? Yes very low.
G            A7    Em7     A7       D G A7 D
What-cha do-in' Jen-  i fer  my love..
```

```
Jen -    i-fer   Jun -  i-per   rides a dappled mare
Jen -    i-fer Jun -    i-per lilacs in her hair..
Is she dreaming? Yes I think so.
Is she pretty? Yes I know so...
What-cha do-in' Jen-  i fer my love?.
```

```
D   A7   D G              A7     G        D
I'm thinkin' of   what it would be like if she loved me...
D   A7   D   F#m          G
F#m 244222
You know just this happy song...
(A6 002222)
G    A7             Em7        A7    A6  A9
It came along and I have to somehow try and ......tell you...
```

UNIVERSAL SOLDIER
Donovan

     C   D   G   Ebm   (Ebm 004342)
He's five foot two and he's six feet four
     C   D   G
He fights with missiles and with spears
     C   D   G   EBm
He's all of thirty-one and he's only seventeen
         Am   D
He's been a soldier for a thousand years
     C   D   G   Ebm
He's a catholic, a hindu, an atheist, a jain,
     C   D   G
A buddhist and a baptist and a jew
     G   D
And he knows he shouldn't kill
     G   Ebm
And he knows he always will
        Am   D
Kill you for me, my friend and me for you
     C   D   G   Ebm
And he's fighting for Canada, he's fighting for France
     C   D G g7
He's fighting for the U.S.A.
     C   D   G   Ebm
He's fighting for the Russians and he's fighting for Japan
     Am   D
And he thinks we'll put an end to war this way
       C   D   G   Ebm
And he's fighting for democracy, he's fighting for the reds

```
       C              D    G                  G7
He says it's for the peace of all
         C            D           G
Ebm
He's the one who must decide who's to live and who's
to die
         Am                       D
```
And he never sees the writing on the wall
But without him how would Hitler have condemned him at Dachau
Without him Caesar would have stood alone
He's the one who gives his body as a weapon of the war
And without him all this killing can't go on
He's the universal soldier and he really is to blame
His orders come from far away no more
They come from here and there and you and me
And brothers can't you see
This is not the way we put the end to war

COLOURS
Donovan

E
Yellow is the color of my true loves hair...
      A   E(riff1)
in the morning when we rise...
      A   E(riff1)
in the morning when we rise...
       B   A   E(riff)
That's the time, thats the time I love the best...

(instrumental Interlude thingie)
 E E A E A E B A   E(It's like the intro till you get to the A chord
then strum)

 Green's the colour of the sprklin' corn
in the morning when we rise
in the morning when we rise
That's the time thats the time I love the best

Mellow is the feelin' that I get
when I see her Mm hmm
when I see her uh - huh
That's the time thats the time I love the best

Freedom .is a word I rarely use...
Without thinkin' mm - hmm
without thinkin' mm -hmm
of the time of the time ....

Outro (its like the intro, you should be able to get it by listening to the song) E   (Comes in on the e or 3).

HURDY GURDY MAN
Donovan

```
G                  Bm            C              D7
```
Thrown like a star in my vast sleep I open my eyes to take a peep
```
G              Bm         C         D7
```
To find that I was by the sea gazing with tranquility
```
        F              C              G
```
'Twas then that the Hurdy Gurdy Man came singing songs of love
```
F                     C            G
D7  G
```
Then when the Hurdy Gurdy Man came singing songs of love

CHORUS
```
F            C              G         D7   G
```
Hurdy gurdy hurdy gurdy hurdy gurdy gurdy he sang
(rereat 3 times)
F C G G

Histories of ages past unenlightened shadows cast
Down through all eternity the crying of humanity
'Tis then that the Hurdy Gurdy Man comes singing songs of love
Then that the Hurdy Gurdy Man comes singing songs of love

Repeat chorus
Repeat 1st line of chorus ad lib to end

OLD FUNNIES

MONSTER MASH
Bobby "Boris" Pickett

   G
I was working in the lab late one night
       Em
When my eyes beheld an eerie sight
   C
For my monster from the slab began to rise
   D
And suddenly, to my surprise
       G
He did the mash He did the Monster Mash
       Em
The Monster Mash It was a graveyard smash
     C
He did the mash It caught on in a flash
     D
He did the mash He did the Monster Mash

From my laboratory in the Castle East
To the Master Bedroom where the vampires feast
The [ghouls all came from their humble abode
To get a jolt from my electrode

And do the mash. And do the Monster Mash
The monster mash. And do my graveyard smash
To do the mash. They caught on in a flash
To do the mash. To do the monster mash

The scene was rocking all were digging the sound
Igor on chains backed by His Baying Hounds
The Coffin Bangers were about to arrive
With their vocal group, the Crypt Kicker Five

ALLEY OOP

   G   - D   - G
Oop Oop,   Oop,   Oop Oop.
      G   - D   - G
Alley Oop Oop,   Oop,   Oop Oop.
        G
There's a man in the funny papers we all know.
                  - D   G
Alley Oop Oop,   Oop,   Oop Oop.
He lived way back a long time ago.
                  - D   G
Alley Oop Oop,   Oop,   Oop Oop.

He don't eat nothin' but a bearcat stew.
                  - D   G
Alley Oop Oop,   Oop,   Oop Oop.
  Well, this cat's name is Alley-Oop.
                  - D   G
Alley Oop Oop,   Oop,   Oop Oop.

He's got a chopper that's a genuine dinosaur.
  Alley Oop Oop,   Oop,   Oop Oop.
  And he can knuckle your head before you count to four.
  Alley Oop Oop,   Oop,   Oop Oop.
  He's got a big ugly club and a head full of hair.
  Alley Oop Oop,   Oop,   Oop Oop.
  Like great big lions and grizzly bears.
  Alley Oop Oop,   Oop,   Oop Oop.
Alley - Oop, he's the toughest man there is alive,
Alley - Oop, wears clothes from a wildcat's hide,
Alley - Oop, he's the king of the jungle jive, look at that
D7
  caveman go!
                   D   G
  Alley Oop Oop, look at that caveman go....

PURPLE PEOPLE EATER
Sheb Wooley

D
Well, I saw the thing comin' out of the sky
   A7   D
It had-a one long horn and one big eye
                         G   D
I commenced to shakin' and I said: "Oooh-Wee
It looks like a Purple People Eater to me."
CHORUS
      D
It was a one-eyed one-horn flyin' Purple People Eater
A7
One-eyed, one-horn, flyin' Purple People Eater
D
One-eyed, one-horn flyin' Purple People Eater
A7   D
Sure looked strange to me. (One Eye?)

Change to [E] (E/A/B7)
Oh, well, he came down to earth and he lit in a tree
I said: "Mr. Purple People Eater don't eat me."
I heard him say in a voice so gruff:
("I wouldn't eat you 'cause you're so tough.")

It was a one-eyed, one-horn flyin' Purple People Eater
(One-eyed, one-horn, flyin' Purple People Eater)
One-eyed, one-horn flyin' Purple People Eater
Sure looked strange to me. (One Horn?)

WITCH DOCTOR
David Seville & the Chipmunks

Capo 1st fret)
(E)(F#)(G#) or

A   (E)(F#)(G#)
I told the witch doctor I was in love with you
A   (E)(F#)(E)
I told the witch doctor you didn't love me too
E/B   A
And then the witch doctor, he told me what to do
(E)(F#) (G#)
He said that

A   D   A   E   E7
Ooo eee, ooo ah ah - ting tang, walla walla, bing bang
A   D   E   E7   A
Ooo eee, ooo ah ah - ting tang, walla walla, bing bang
Ooo eee, ooo ah ah - ting tang, walla walla, bing bang
Ooo eee, ooo ah ah - ting tang, walla walla, bing bang

(Capo 2nd fret)

I told the witch doctor you didn't love me true
I told the witch doctor you didn't love me nice
And then the witch doctor, he game me this advice
He said to

Ooo eee, ooo ah ah - ting tang, walla walla, bing bang
Ooo eee, ooo ah ah - ting tang, walla walla, bing bang
Ooo eee, ooo ah ah - ting tang, walla walla, bing bang
Ooo eee, ooo ah ah - ting tang, walla walla, bing bang

ITSY BITSY TEENY WEENY YELLOW POLHA DOT BIKINI
(by Lee Pockriss & Paul Vance)

She was afraid to come out of the locker,
She was as nervous as she could be.
She was afraid to come out of the locker.
She was afraid that somebody would see.

Two, three, four, tell the people what she wore.

It was an itsy bitsy teeny weeny yellow polka dot bikini,
That she wore for the first time today,
An itsy teeny weeny yellow polka dot bikini,
So in the locker she wanted to stay.

Two, three, four, stick around we'll tell you more.

She was afraid to come out of the blanket,
She was as nervous as she could be.
She was afraid to come out of the blanket.
She was afraid that somebody would see.

Two, three, four, tell the people what she wore.

It was an itsy bitsy teeny weeny yellow polka dot bikini,
That she wore for the first time today,
An itsy teeny weeny yellow polka dot bikini,
So in the blanket she wanted to stay.

Two, three, four, stick around we'll tell you more.

TIE ME KANGAROO DOWN, SPORT
Rolf Harris

D   G
Watch me wallaby's feed, mate,
A   D
Watch me wallaby's feed,
D   G
They're a dangerous breed, mate,
  A   D
So watch me wallaby's feed.
CHORUS:
    A
Altogether now
D   G
Tie me kangaroo down, sport,
A   D
Tie me kangaroo down.
D   G
Tie me kangaroo down, sport,
A   D
Tie me kangaroo down.

Keep me cockatoo cool, Curl, Keep me cockatoo cool.
Don't go acting the fool, Curl, Just keep me cockatoo cool.
(CHORUS)

Take me koala back, Jack, Take me koala back.
He lives somewhere out on the track, Mac,
So take me Koala back.
(CHORUS)

ROCKIN

&

ROLLIN

SWEET GEORGIA BROWN
by Louis Armstrong

RUN: G Gb F (all in F config) then to E7

E7
No gal made has got a shade on Sweet Georgia Brown,
A7
Two left feet, oh, so neat, Has Sweet Georgia Brown
D7
They all sigh, and want to die, For Sweet Georgia Brown!
D7   G   D7   G   RUN
I'll tell you just why, You know I don't lie, not much
E7
It's been said She knocks 'em dead, When she lands in town!
A7
Since she came, Why it's a shame, How she cools them down!
Em   B7   Em   B7
Fellows she can't get Are fellows she aint met
 G   Bb   F   E7
Georgia claimed her, Georgia named her,
A7   D7   G
Sweet Georgia Brown!

No gal made has got a shade on Sweet Georgia Brown,
Two left feet, oh, so neat, Has Sweet Georgia Brown!
They all sigh, and want to die, For Sweet Georgia Brown!
I'll tell you just why, You know I don't lie, not much

All those gifts some courters give, To Sweet Georgia Brown,
They buy clothes at fashion shows, With one dollar down,
Oh, boy! Tip your hat! Oh, joy She's the cat!

Who's that, Mister? Tain't a Sister!
Sweet Georgia Brown

BOOK OF LOVE.

```
   F       Dm            Gm7                  C7
Tell me, tell me, tell me, Oh who  wrote the book of love
      F          Dm           Gm7           C7
I've got to know the answer, Was it someone from above
     F              Bb                         F
I wonder wonder who,  who, Who wrote the book of love
         Dm    Gm7         C7
I love you darling baby, you know I do
      F          Dm          Gm7              C7
But I've got to see this book of love, Find out why it's true
F               Bb                         F
I wonder wonder who,  who, Who wrote the book of love
Bb                F
Chapter one says to love her To love her with all your heart
Bb               C7
Chapter two you tell her, Your never, never, never ever
          gonna part
     F       Dm           Gm7    C7
In chapter three remember the meaning of romance
      F           Dm           Gm7
In chapter four you break up, But you give just one more
         chance
     F                Bb                           F
Oh I wonder wonder who,  who, Who wrote the book of love
F       Dm       Gm7      C7
Baby baby baby, I love you yes I do,
        F         Dm
Well it says so in the Book of Love
Gm7            C7
Ours is the one that's true,
F               Bb                     F
I wonder wonder who Who wrote the book of love
```

249

PARTY DOLL

G
Well all I want is a party doll,
    D   G
To come along with me when I'm feelin' wild,

To be everlovin', true and fair,
    D   G
To run her fingers through my hair.

CHORUS
G
Come along and be my party doll,
D   G
Come along and be my party doll,
                      C
Come along and be my party doll,
    D   G
I wanna make love to you, to you,
    D   G
I wanna make love to you.

Well I saw a gal walkin' down the street,
The kind of a gal I'd love to meet,
She had blonde hair and eyes of blue,
Baby I wanna have a party with you.
CHORUS

Every man has got to have a party doll,
To be with him when he's feelin' wild,
To be everlovin', true and fair
To run her fingers through his hair,
To run her fingers through his hair.
CHORUS

DOWN BY THE STATION

G   D7   G
Down by the station, early in the morning
                    D7   G
I met a little girl as cute a she could be
              Em   C   D7
I turned on my charm and told her I loved her
G   D7   G
I told that she always be the number one for me
G   C   D7   G   C
She'd always be my number one girl
G   D7   G
I said there' be no number two or three

Down by malt shop shortly thereafter
I met another girl about as cute as she could be
I looked for number one and when I could see her
I told number two she was the only girl for me

Went to the drugstore, nearly lost my life there
I saw my little girls friends one and two
Standin' there together, I knew I was in trouble,
 I'se a clever fellow, I knew what to do

I went on down by the station early in the mornin'
I was with a through with women as cute as they could be
But then I saw another girl a lookin' kind of pretty
I said I'm through with one and two, I love you number three
Here's what she said to me

Down by the station, early in the morning
See the little pufferbellies all in a row
See the station master pull the little handle
Chug Chug Toot Toot Off they go
Chug Chug Toot Toot Off they go

KISSES SWEETER THAN WINE

```
Dm              C            Dm
When I was a young man and never been kissed
            C          Dm
I got to thinking it over what I had missed.
                C              Am          Dm
I got me a girl, I kissed her and then, Oh lord, I kissed her again
```

CHORUS
```
Dm   C          Dm        C             Dm
Oh, kisses sweeter than wine, Oh, kisses sweeter than wine
```

I asked her to marry and be my sweet wife,
And we would be so happy the rest of our lives.
I begged and I pleaded like a natural man,
And then, Oh Lord, she gave me her hand.
CHORUS

I worked mighty hard and so did my wife,
Workin' hand in hand to make a good life.
With corn in the field and wheat in the bins,
I was, Oh Lord, the father of twins.
CHORUS

Our children they numbered just about four,
They all had sweethearts knockin' at the door.
They all got married and they didn't hesitate;
I was, Oh Lord, the grandmother of eight.
CHORUS

 Now that we're old, and ready to go,
We get to thinkin' what happened a long time ago.
We had a lot of kids, trouble and pain,
But, Oh Lord, We'd do it again.

SINGING THE BLUES
(Van Morrison)

```
G                          C
Well, I never felt more like singin' the blues
     G                 D7         C
'cause I never thought that I'd ever lose your lovin'
         D7       G
You got me singin' the blues
 G                         C
Well, I never felt more like cryin' all night
    G                       D7              C
'cause ev'rythings wrong an' nothin' ain't right without you
         D7       G
You got me singin' the blues
```

CHORUS
```
    C                     G
The moon and stars no longer shine
    C               G
A dream is gone I thought was mine
    C         G
Nothin' left for me to do
              D
But cry-i-i-i over you
```

Well, I never felt more like runnin' away, But why should I go?
'cause I couldn't stay without you, You got me singin' the blues
CHORUS

I never felt more like runnin' away, But why should I go?
'cause I couldn't stay without you, You got me singin' the blues
CHORUS
You got me singin' the blues, You got me singin' the blues

BAD BAD LEROY BROWN
(Jim Croce)

              G   A7
Well the South side of Chicago Is the baddest part of town
      B7   C
And if you go down there, You better just beware
   D7   G
Of a man named Leroy Brown, Now Leroy's more than trouble,
               A7
You see, he stands about six foot four
      B7   C
All those down-town ladies, Call him treetop lover
   D7   G
All the men just call him Sir

REFRAIN
      G
And he's bad, bad Leroy Brown,
  A7
Baddest man in the whole damn town
  B7   C
Badder than old King Kong,
     D   C   G
And meaner than a junkyard dog

Now Leroy, he's a gambler, And he likes his fancy clothes
And he likes to wear, His diamond rings
In front of everybody's nose

He's got a custom Continental, He's got an El Dorado, too
He's got a .32 gun, In his pocket for fun
He got a razor in his shoe

HONEYCOMB
by Jimmy Rogers

         C   C7
Well, it's a darn good life and it's kinda funny,
      F
How the Lord made the bee and the bee made the honey,
      G   C
And the honeybee was lookin' for home (break) And they called it honeycomb, 'n 'ey
C
Roamed the world and they gathered all of the
F
Honeycomb into one sweet ball, and the
G   C
Honeycomb from a million trips made my baby's lips, oh

CHORUS

F
Honeycomb, a-won't you be my baby? Well,
C
honeycomb be my own?
     G7
Got a hank of hair and a piece of bone,
           C
And made a break) walkin', talkin' honeycomb, well
F
Honeycomb, won't you be my baby?
C
Well a-honeycomb be my own?
     G7   C
What a darn good life when you got a wife like a-honeycomb.

ALL I HAVE TO DO IS DREAM
Everly Brothers

```
     C      Am    Dm7    G7
When I Want You  In My Arms
   C      Am     Dm        G7
when I want you   and all your charms
   C         Am
whenever i want you
F        G7    C    Am     F       G7
all li have to do is dream, dream, dream, dream.

   C      Am    Dm     G7
when li feel blue  in the night
   C     Am   Dm       G7
and I need you  to hold me tight
    C         Am
 whenever I want you
F        G7     C    F  C   C7
all I have to do is dream.

F                    Em
I can make you mine  taste your lips of wine
Dm    G7      C    C7
anytime  night or day.
F            Em
only trouble is  gee whiz,
        D7         G7
I'm dreaming my life away.

   C    Am  Dm     G7
I need you so   that li could die.
   C     Am  Dm      G7
I love you so   and that is why.
        C       Am      F       G7    C   F   C
Whenever I want you all I have to is dream#
```

BYE BYE LOVE
The Everly Brothers

```
F         C    F       C
```
Bye bye love bye bye happiness
```
F    C                      G7
```
Hello loneliness I think I'm gonna cr-y
```
F         C    F       C
```
Bye bye love bye bye sweet caress
```
F    C                      G7   C
```
Hello emptiness I feel like I could d-ie
```
    G7            C
```
Bye my love good-by


```
              G7                    C
```
There goes my baby with someone new
```
              G7          C
```
She sure looks happy I sure am blue
```
      C7   F              G7
```
She was my baby till he stepped in
```
                                 C
```
Goodbye to romance that might have been

repeat #1
```
              G7                        C
```
I'm through with romance I'm through with love
```
              G7            C
```
I'm through with counting the stars above
```
      C7   F              G7
```
And here's the reason that I'm so free
```
                           C
```
My loving baby is through with me

257

BE-BOP-A-LULA:
Everly Brothers.

INTRO:
A
Be-bop-a-lula she's my baby,
Be-bop-a-lula I don't mean maybe,
D
Be-bop-a-lula she's my baby,
A
Be-bop-a-lula I don't mean maybe,
E   A   E
Be-bop-a-lula she's my baby doll, my baby doll, my baby doll

A
She's the gal in the red blue jeans,
She's the queen of all the teens,
        A7
She's the one that I know,
A   A7
She's the one that love's me so.

CHORUS:
     D   A
Be-bop-a-lula she's my baby, be-bop-a-lula I don't
           E   A
mean maybe, be-bop-a-lula she's my baby doll, my baby doll,
     E
my baby doll.

I KISSED YA
Everly Brothers.

INTRO: F Dm (x2)

F　　Dm　　　　　　F　　　Dm
Never felt like this until I kissed ya.
F　　Dm　　　F　　　Dm
How did I exist until I kissed ya.
F
Never had you on my mind,
C7　　　　　　　　C　　C7
Now you're there all the time.
F　　Dm　　　　　　　　F　　　　Dm
Never knew what I missed til I kissed ya, uh-huh,
F　　　　Dm
I kissed ya, whoaa, yeah.

CHORUS:
Dm　　　　　　　　　　F
You don't realize what you do to me.
　Dm　　　　　　　　F
And I didn't realize what a kiss could be.

OUTRO:
　F　　　　Dm　　　　　F　　　Dm
I kissed ya, whoaa, yeah..I kissed ya, uh-huh..
F
I KISSED YA!

JONNY IS A JOKER
The Everly Brothers

INTRO B   E A F# 2 times
       / / / / / / / /

B
Johnny, he's a joker (he's a bird)
A very funny joker (he's a bird)
    E
But when he jokes my honey (he's a dog)
   B
His jokin' ain't so funny (what a dog)
F#   E
Johnny is a joker that's a-tryin' to steal my baby
        B   E   A F# [as per intro]
(He's a bird dog)

E
Hey, Bird Dog, get away from my quail
B
Hey, Bird Dog, you're on the wrong trail
F#   E   B7
Bird Dog you better leave my lovey-dove alone
E
Hey, Bird Dog, get away from my chick
B
Hey, Bird Dog, you better get away quick
F#   E   B
Bird Dog, you better find a Chicken Little of your own

WAKE UP LITTLE SUSIE
The Everly Brothers

D F G F D F G F D F G F D F G F
D   F G F
Wake up little Susie, wake up
D   F G F
Wake up little Susie, wake up
     G   D   G   G   D   G
The movie wasn't so hot, it didn't have much of a plot
 G   D   G   D   G D G
We fell asleep, our goose is cooked, our reputation is shot
          A   G   A
Wake up little Susie, wake up little Susie
CHORUS:
A   G   A
What are you gonna tell your mamma?
A   G   A
What are you gonna tell your pa?
A   G   A   N.C.
What are we gonna tell our friends when they say "ooh la la"?
         D A   D
Wake up little Susie, wake up little Susie
    D
Well I told your momma that you'd be home by ten
      G
Well now Susie baby looks like we goofed again
         A G   A (N.C.)
Wake up little Susie, wake up little Susie,
     D F G F
we gotta go home

YOUNG LOVE
Sonny James

INTRO: C - Am - F - G

C
 They say for every boy and girl,
      E7
There's just one love in this old world,
   F   G   C   Am F G
And I, I know, I, I, I've found mine,
C
 The heavenly touch of your embrace,
E7
Tells me no one will take your place,
F G   C   Am F G
 e-e-e-ver in my heart,
C   G7   F#
Young love, first love,
F   G   C   Am F G
Filled with true devo--tion,
C   G7   F#
Young love, our (love,
  F   G   C   Am F G
We share with deep emo-tion, /Am F G,

YOUNG LOVE

C   Am
They say for every boy and girl
     F   G
There's just one love in this whole world
C   Am
And I know I've found mine
C   Am
The heavenly touch of your embrace
F   G
Tells me no one could take your place
     C
Ever in my heart
CHORUS
 C   G7 F   C
Young love, first love Filled with true devotion
 C   G7 F   C
Young love, our love, we share with deep emotion

Just one kiss from your sweet lips
Will tell me that your love is real
And I can feel that it's true
We will vow to one another
There will never be another
Love for you or for me
CHORUS

IT'S SO EASY
Buddy Holly, Norman Petty

A   E   D   E
It's so easy to fall in love,
A   D   E   A
It's so easy to fall in love
A   E   D   E
People tell me love's for fools,
A   D   E   A
So here I go breaking all of the rules

A   D
It seems so easy, (seems so easy, seems so easy)
D   A
Umm-hmm so doggone easy (doggone easy , doggone easy)
A   D
Umm-hmm, it seems so easy, (seems so easy, seems so easy, seems so easy)
D B7   E7
Well, your concerned that my heart has learned

PEGGY SUE
Buddy Holly

```
A        D        A        D        A
If you knew Peggy Sue, then you'd know why I feel blue
    D                A   D A E
About Peggy, 'bout Peggy Sue
        E             D            A   D A E
Oh, well, I love you gal, yes, I love you Peggy Sue.

A                         F
Peggy Sue, Peggy Sue, pretty, pretty, pretty, pretty,
    A
Peggy Sue,
        D            A    D A E
Oh, my Peggy, my Peggy Sue
        E             D             A   D A E
Oh, well, I love you gal, and I need you, Peggy Sue.
```

RAVE ON
Buddy Holly *

       E
A-well the little things you say and do, they make me want to be with you
E7 A   E   B7
hoo. Rave on, it's a crazy feeling and I know it's got me reeling when you
           E A E B7
say, 'I love you,' rave on.
  E
The way you dance and hold me tight, the way you kiss and say good-ni-hi-
E7 A   E   B7
hight; Rave on, it's a crazy felling and I know it's got me reeling when you
        E A E B7
say, 'I love you,' rave on.

     A   E   B7
A-well rave on, it's a crazy felling and I know it's got me reeling I'm so
                      E B7 E E7 A7
glad that you're revealing your love for me! Rave on, rave on and tell me,
E   B7   E
tell me not to be lonely, tell me your love me only rave
A   E
on me, rave on to me

THAT'LL BE THE DAY
Buddy Holly

[D]
Well, that'll be the day When you say good-bye
[A]
Yes, that'll be the day When you make me cry
[D]
You say you're gonna leave You know it's a lie
[A]   [E7]   [A]
'cause that'll be the day when I die
[E7] [A]
When I die

[D]   [A]
Well, you give me all your lovin' and your turtle dovin'
[D]   [A]
All your hugs and kisses and your money too
[D]   [A]
Well, you know you love me baby, still you tell me
[B7]   [E7]
That someday well I'll be blue

[D]
Well, that ll be the day, woo hoo
[A]
Well, that ll be the day, woo hoo
[D]
Well, that ll be the day, woo hoo
[A]
That ll be the day

WELL ALRIGHT
Buddy Holly

Capo II E D E 2x

       E   D   E
Well, alright so I'm being foolish,
              D   E
well, alright let people know
                     D   E
About the dreams and wishes you wish,
                 B*   E
and the night when lights are low

   A   B
Well alright, well alright,
      E   D   E
we will live and love with all our might
A   B
Well alright, well alright,
     E   D   E
our lifetime's love will be alright

BLUE SUEDE SHOES
Elvis Presley

A
Well it's a one for the money, two for the show,
                      A7
three to get ready now go, cat ,go,
     D   A
but don't you step on my blue suede shoes.
       E   D   A
You can do anything, but lay off of my blue suede shoes.

    A
Well you can knock me down, step in my face, slander my name all over the place, and do anything that you want to do.

But ah ah, honey, lay off of my shoes
    D   A
and don't you step on my blue suede shoes.
      E   D   A
You can do anything, but lay off of my blue suede shoes.

        A
It`s blue blue, blue suede shoes, blue blue, blue suede shoes,
D   A
blue blue, blue suede shoes, baby,   blue blue, blue suede shoes.
       E   D   A
Well, you can do anything but lay off of my blue suede shoes.

CHANTILLY LACE
The Big Bopper

Intro: G C G C C7 F C G C

       G
Chantilly lace and a pretty face
      C
And a ponytail a-hangin' down
          G
That wiggle in the walk and giggle in the talk
C   C7
Makes the world go round
       F
There ain't nothin' in the world like a big-eyed girl
    C
That makes me act so funny, makes me spend my money
G
Makes me feel real loose like a long-necked goose
C [stop]
Like a girl, oh baby, that's what I like

G   C
What's that baby?
     G   C
But, but, but
  C7   F
Ohhh honey
      C   G   C
But...oh, baby, you know what I like

WHITE LIGHTENING
J.P. Richardson (The Big Booper)

E
In North Carolina, way back in the hills,

there lived my Pappy and he had him a still.
    A
He brewed white lightning till the sun was down,
           E
and then he'd fill him a jug, and pass it around.
B   A
Mighty, mighty pleasin', my Pappy's corn squeezin'..
    E
called, white Lightning.

CHORUS:
A
G-men, T-men, Revenurers too,
E
searchin' for the place where he made his brew.
         B
They were lookin', tryin' to book him,
      A   E   B
But my Pappy kept on cookin'..white Lightning.

I asked my Pappy why he called his brew..
white lightning, instead of mountain dew.
I took one sip and then I knew,
as my eyes bugged out and my face turned blue.
Mighty, mighty pleasin', my Pappy's corn squeezin'..
called..white Lightning.

HOUND DOG
Elvis Presley

                              G
You ain't nothing but a hound dog - Crying all the time
                           C7
You ain't nothing but a hound dog - Crying all the time
              D7   C7   G
Well, you ain't never caught a rabbit and you ain't no friends of mine

                      G
They said you was high-classed

but that was just a lie
                      C7
They said you was high-classed
                  G
but that was just a lie
              D7
Well, you ain't never caught a rabbit
     C7   G
and you ain't no friends of mine

SINGING THE BLUES
Elvis Presley

[C] Well, I never felt more like singin' the [F] blues
[C] 'Cause I never thought that I'd ever [G] lose
[C] Your [F] love [G] dear, why'd you do me this [C] way

Well, I never felt more like cryin' all [F] night
[C] 'Cause everything's wrong, there ain't nothin' [G] right
[C] With-[F] out [G] you, you got me singin' the [C] blues.

[F] Now the moon and stars no [C] longer shine
[F] The dream is gone I [C] thought was mine
[F] There's nothin' left for [C] me to do
But Cry-y-y [G] over you (cry over you)

[C] Well, I never felt more like runnin' [F] away
[C] But how can I go when I couldn't [G] stay
[C] With-[F] out [G] you, you got me singin' the [C] blues.

JAILHOUSE ROCK
Recorded by Elvis Presley

C
The warden threw a party in the county jail

The prison band was there and they began to wail

The band was jumping and the joint began to swing
                                          C7
You should've heard those knocked out jailbirds sing

F   C
Let's rock everybody let's rock
G7   F
Everybody in the whole cell block
   C
Was dancing to the Jailhouse Rock

Spider Murphy played the tenor saxophone
Little Joe was blowing on the slide trombone
The drummer boy from Illinois went crash boom bang
The whole rhythm section was the Purple Gang

Number forty seven said to number three
You're the cutest jailbird I ever did see
I sure would be delighted with your company
Come on and do the Jailhouse Rock with me

Shifty Henry said to Bugs for heaven's sake
No one's looking nows our chance to make a break
Bugs turned to Shifty and he said nix nix
I wanna stick around a while and get my kicks

JOHNNY B GOODE
Written by Chuck Berry

INTRO: A   E D A

A
Deep down in Louisianna, Close to New Orleans

Way back up in the woods, among the evergreens
      D
There stand a country cabin, made of clay and wood
    A
Where lives a young country boy, named Johnny B. Goode
  E
He never ever learned to read or write a book so well
        A
But he could play his guitar, just like a-ringing a bell

   A
Go go, go Johnny go go go!
          D
Go Johnny go go go!
          A
Go Johnny go go go!
          E
Go Johnny go go go!
      A
Aah Johnny B. Goode!

GUITAR SOLO: A D A   D   A   E   A E **X2**

LOVE POTION NUMER 9
The Searchers

Am   Dm
I took my troubles down to Madame Rue
Am   Dm
You know that gypsy with the gold-capped tooth
C   Am
She's got a pad down on Thirty-Fourth and Vine
Dm   E   Am
Sellin' little bottles of Love Potion Number Nine

Dm
She bent down and turned around and gave me a wink
      B7
She said "I'm gonna make it up right here in the sink"
       Dm
It smelled like turpentine, it looked like Indian ink
    E
I held my nose, I closed my eyes, I took a drink
Am   Dm
I didn't know if it was day or night
Am   Dm
I started kissin' everything in sight
C   Am
But when I kissed a cop down on Thirty-Fourth and Vine
Dm   E   Am
He broke my little bottle of Love Potion Number Nine
Dm   Am
Love Potion Number Nine 3x

ONLY THE LONELY
recorded by Roy Orbison

G   Am
Only the lonely know the way I feel tonight
D7   C   G
Only the lonely know this feeling ain't right
                             C
There goes my baby there goes my heart
                A7   D7
They've gone forever so far apart
          G   C   D7   G
But only the lonely know why I cry only the lonely

                                              Am
Only the lonely know the heartaches I've been through
D7   C   G
Only the lonely know I cry and cry for you
                   C
Maybe tomorrow on new romance
                        A7
No more sorrow but that's the chance
D7   C   D7
You've got to take if your lonely heart breaks
       G   D7   G
Only the lonely   only the lonely

BOOK OF LOVE

[C] They say for every [F] boy there's a [C] girl
And she's [F] waitin' somewhere in [C] this world
It's [F] all been planned to [E7] someone up a[Am]bove [F]
And [C] I know it's [F] written in the [G7] book of [C] love

[F] Written there for [E7] all the world to [Am] see
[F] Written there to [G7] last eter[C]nally
[F] Night and day it's [E7] you I'm dreaming [Am] of [F]
And [C] I know our [F] names are in that [G7] book of [C] love

Now I [F] love you since the [C] day we met
Really [F] love you without a [C] reason or regret
[F] Night and day it's [E7] you I'm dreaming [Am] of [F]
And [C] I know our [F] names are in that [G7] book of [C] love

[F] Night and day it's [E7] you I'm dreaming [Am] of [F]
And [C] I know our [F] names are in that [G7] book of [C] love [Am]
[C] Yes I know our [F] names are in that [G7] book of [C] love

278

SAVE THE LAST DANCE FOR ME
Michael Buble

        D   A
You can dance, every dance for the guy who gives you the eye, let him hold you tight.
    A
You can smile, every smile for the man who held your
D
hand 'neath the pale moonlight.

CHORUS
D   G
But dont forget whos takin' you home and in whos
    D
arms you're gonna be.
A   D
sooo darlin save the last dance for me.
D
Oh I no, that the music's fine like sparkin' wine go
A
and have your fun.
A
Laugh and sing, but while where apart dont give your
D
heart to anyone.

CHORUS AGAIN

THE ALL AMERICAN BOY
(Bobby Bare)

(SPOKEN IN A SING-SONG PATTER RATHER THAN SUNG)
```
G                         C
Gather 'round, cats, and I'll tell you a story
      D                       G
About how to become an All American Boy
                      C
Buy you a gittar and put it in tune
  D             G
You'll be rockin' and rollin' soon.
```
Impressin' the girls, pickin' hot licks, and all that jazz

I-I bought me a gittar a year ago
Learned how to play in a day or so
And all around town it was well understood
That I was knockin' 'em out like Johnny B. Goode
Hot licks, showin' off, ah number one.

Well, I'd practice all day and up into the night
My papa's hair was turnin' white
Cause he didn't like rock'n'roll
He said "You can stay, boy, but that's gotta go."
He's a square, he just didn't dig me at all

So I took my gittar, picks and all
And bid farewell to my poor ole pa
And I split for Memphis where they say all
Them swingin' cats are havin' a ball
Sessions, hot licks and all, they dig me

THE ALL AMERICAN BOY
(Bobby Bare)

I was rockin' and boppin' and I's a gettin' the breaks
The girls all said that I had what it takes
When up stepped a man with a big cigar
He said "come here, cat--I'm gonnna make you a star."
"I'll put you on Bandstand, buy ya a Cadillac, sign here, kid."

I signed my name and became a star
Havin' a ball with my gittar
Driving a big long Cadillac and fightin' the girls off ma back
They just kept a'comin', screamin', yeah-they like it

So I'd pick my gittar with a great big grin
And the money just kept on pourin' in
But then one day my Uncle Sam
He said (sound of 3 footsteps) "Here I am"
"Uncle Sam needs you, boy
I'm-a gonna cut your hair
ah-Take this rifle, kid
Gimme that gittar" yeah.

TRY TO REMEMBER
(Tom Jones)

```
    G                   Am        D7
Try to remember the kind of September
    G                Am      D7
when life was slow and oh, so mellow.
 G                      Am        D7
Try to remember the kind of September
    G                   A7        D7
 when grass was green and grain was yellow.
Bm7     Em7     Am7       D7
Try to remember the kind of September
           Gmaj7    Cmaj7    F        D7
when you were a tender and callow fellow,
 G                 Am        D7       G
Try to remember and if you remember the follow.
```

Try to remember when life was so tender
that no one wept except the willow.
Try to remember when life was so tender that
dreams were kept beside your pillow.
Try to remember when life was so tender that
love was an ember about to billow.
Try to remember and if you remember then follow.

Deep in December it's nice to remember
altho you know the snow will follow.
Deep in December it's nice to remember
without the hurt the heart is hollow.
Deep in December it's nice to remember
the fire of September that made us mellow.
Deep in December our hearts should remember and follow.

CHORDS
Gmaj7 320002   Am7   002213   Cmaj7 032000
Em7   022030   Bm7   024232

DOWNTOWN
(Petula Clark)

```
G            Gmaj7           C             D7
```
When you're alone, And life is making you lonely,
```
         G      C    D       G             Gmaj7
```
You can always go downtown, When you've got worries,
```
         C            D7           G       C       D
```
All the noise and the hurry, Seems to help, I know, downtown

```
     G                        Em
```
Just listen to the music of the traffic in the city
```
    G                          Em
```
Linger on the sidewalk where the neon signs are pretty
```
     Bm
```
How can you lose?

CHORUS
```
C
```
The lights are much brighter there
```
         Em7              Em7          A
```
You can forget all your troubles, forget all your cares and go
```
   G   Gmaj7 Am7   D6         Am
```
Downtown, things'll be great when you're
```
   C  Dmaj7 Am7   D6         Am
```
Downtown, no finer place for sure
```
   G   Dmaj7   Am7  D6        Am    G
```
Downtown, everything's waiting for you

Don't hang around, And let your problems surround you
There are movie shows downtown
Maybe you know Some little places to go to
Where they never close downtown

Just listen to the rhythm of a gentle bossanova
You'll be dancing with 'em too before the night is over
Happy again

LOOK WHAT THEY'VE DONE TO MY SONG

Hello mama, hello mama it's me, How you feeling mama?
Hm-hmm, that's alright, I've got something I want to talk to you about
If you don't mind, And I ain't mad, mama, no, no no no, Wait a minute, listen mama

 C   Am
Look what they done to my song, ma
 F
Look what they done to my song, ma
     C   D
The only thing I could do half right
             F
and now it's turning out all wrong, mama
 C   G   C
Look what they done to my song

KOKOMO by The Beach Boys

C   F
Aruba, Jamaica, ew I wanna take ya, Bermuda, Bahama, come on pretty mama
 C   F
Key Largo, Montego, baby why don't we go, Jamaica...
   C   Em
Off the Florida Keys
Gm   F   Fm   (Fm 133111)
There's a place called Kokomo
         C   Dm   G
That's where you wanna go to get away from it all
      Em
Bodies in the sand
Gm   F   Fm   (Gm 000333)
Tropical drink melting in your hand
        C   Dm   G
We'll be falling in love to the rhythm of a steel drum band, Down in Kokomo...

CHORUS
C   F
Aruba, Jamaica, ew I wanna take ya to Bermuda, Bahama, come on pretty mama
  C   F
Key Largo Montego...Ew I wanna take her down to Kokomo,
  Fm   C
We'll get there fast & then we'll take slow
Am   F   G
That's where we wanna go
          C
Way down in Koko...Martinique, that Monserate mystique

TAKIN CARE OF BUSINESS

G   F
You wake up every morning from the alarm clocks warning,
   C   G
And take the 8:15 to the city.

                                        F
There's a whistle up above and people pushing people shoving,
   C   G
And girls, who try to look pretty.

And if your trains on time, you can get to work by 9.
And start your slaving job and get your pay.
If you ever get annoyed, look at me I'm self employed,
I love to work at nothing all day. And I'll be...

Taking care of business, every day.
Taking care of business, every way.
I've been taking care of business, it's all mine.
Taking care of business, and working over time, work out.

It's as easy as fishin', you can be a musican.
If you can make sounds that are mellow.
Get a second hand guitar, chances are you'll go far,
If you hangin out with the right bunch of fellows.

People will see you having fun, just lying in the sun.
Tell them that you like it this way.
It's the work that we avoid, and we're all self employed,
We love to work at nothing all day. And I'll be...

AMERICAN PIE

CHORUS
*   G   C   G   D*
So bye bye, Miss American Pie
*   G   C   G   D*
Drove my Chevy to the levee, But the levee was dry
*   G   c   g   D*
Them good ole boys were drinkin whiskey and rye
*   Em   A7 Em   D7*
Singin' this'll be the day that I die This'll be the day that I die

G   Am   C   Am
Did you write the book of love and do you have faith in god above
Em   D   G   D   Em
If the Bible tells you so, Now do you believe in rock and roll
     Am7   C
Can music save your mortal soul
        Em   A7   D
And can you teach me how to dance real slow?
     Em   D
Well I know that you're in love with him cause
 Em   D   C   G   A7
I saw you dancing in the gym You both kicked off your shoes
     C   D7
Man I dig those rhythm and blues
    G   D   Em
I was a lonely teenage bronc in' buck
    Am   C
with a pink carnation and a pickup truck.
  G   D   Em   C   D7   C
But I knew I was out of luck the day the music died
G   D7
I started singin' ……..
CHORUS

XMAS FAVORITES

GOD REST YE MERRY GENTLEMEN

```
     Em    B7   Em           C           B7
God rest ye merry gentlemen, let nothing you dismay.
     Em    B7         Em     C           B7
Remember Christ our Saviour was born on Christmas
Day,
    Am         G    B7         Em         D
 to save us all from Satan's power, when we were gone
astray.
    G       Em  B7    Em  A7      D
  O tidings of comfort and joy, comfort and joy,
    G       Em B7        Em
 o tidings of comfort and joy.
```

From God our heavenly Father, a blessed angel came,
  and unto certain shepherds brought tidings of the
same,
   How that in Bethlehem was born the Son of God by
name,
   O tidings of comfort and joy, comfort and joy,
   o tidings of comfort and joy.

GOOD KING WENCESLAS

```
 G          Em                  C              G
Good King Wenceslas looked out on the Feast of Stephen,
 G             Em           C              G
  when the snow lay 'round about, deep and crisp and even.
 G                Em          C            G
   Brightly shone the moon that night, though the frost was cruel,
 G              Em            D         EmCG
   when a poor man came in sight, gath'ring winter fu…..el.
```

Hither, page, and stand by me, if thou know'st it, telling
Yonder peasant, who is he? Where and what his dwelling?
Sire, he lives a good league hence, underneath the mountain.
 Right against the forest fence by Saint Agnes' foun…tain.

Bring me flesh and bring me wine, bring me pine logs hither.
Thou and I shall see him dine, when we bear them thither.
 Page and monarch, forth they went, forth they went together,
 through the rude wind's wild lament and the bitter wea…ther.

HARK THE HEROLD ANGELS SING

  G   Am   G   C   D7   G
Hark! The herold angels sing, glory to the new-born king:
G   Em   A7 D   A7 D
 Peace on earth and mercy mild, God and sinners reconciled.
G   D7 G   D7
Joyful all the nations rise, join the triumph of the skies,
C   E7   AmG   D7   G   D7 G
With the angelic host proclaim, Christ is born in Bethlehem!
C   E7   Am   D7 G   D7   G
<u>**Hark! The herold angels sing, glory to the new-born king.**</u>

 Christ, by highest heaven adored,
Christ, the everlasting Lord,
Late in tie behold him come,
Offspring of a virgin`s womb.
 Veiled in flesh the Godhead see,
Hail th`incarnate deity,
Pleased as man with man to dwell,
Jesus our Emmanuel.

HAVE YOURSELF A MERRY LITTLE CHRISTMAS

INTRO G - C - Am - D7

G   Em   Am   D7
 Have yourself a merry little Christmas,
G   Em   Am   - D7
Let your heart be light,
G   Em   Am   D7   - E7   A7-D7
From now on your troubles will be out of sight.

 G   Em   Am   D7
 Have yourself a merry little Christmas,
G   Em   Am   - D7
Make the Yuletide gay,
G   Em   Am   B7   Em   - G
Next year all our troubles will be miles away.

Em   D
Once again as in olden days
     Am   D7   C#7
Happy golden days   of yore,
Em   Bm   - E
Faithful friends who are dear to us
       D   Am   D7
Will be near to us once more.

IT CAME UPON A MIDNIGHT CLEAR

    G   C   G
It came upon the midnight clear,
 C   A7   D - D7
That glorious song of old,
       G   C   C
From angels bending near the earth
 C   D   G
To touch their harps of gold.
     B7   Em
Peace on the earth, good will to men,
     A   A7   D- D7
From heaven's all gracious King !"
    G   C   G
The world in solemn stillness lay
    C   D   G
To hear the angels sing.

Still through the cloven skies they come with peaceful wings unfurled,
And still their heavenly music floats all o'er the weary world.
Above its sad and lowly plains they bend on hovering wing,
And ever o'er its Babel sounds the blessed angels sing.

HERE COMES SANTA CLAUS

  C
Here comes Santa Claus, here comes Santa Claus,
  G   G7
Right down Santa Claus Lane,
  G   G7
He's got a bag that is filled with toys
     C   C7
For boys and girls again.
 F   Em
Hear those sleigh bells jingle jangle,
Dm   C
Oh, what a beautiful sight.
  F   C   A7
So, jump in bed, and cover your head,
    G7   C - D
Cause Santa Claus comes tonight.

Here comes Santa Claus,
Here comes Santa Claus,
Right down Santa Claus Lane,
He doesn't care if you're rich or poor
So fill your hearts with Christmas cheer,
Cause Santa Claus comes tonight !

IT'S BEGINNING TO LOOK LIKE CHRISTMAS

[G] It's beginning to look a lot like [C] Christ[G]mas,
[G7] Ev'rywhere you [C - E] go,
[C] Take a look in the five and [D] ten,
[D7] Glistening once a[G]gain
[D] With candy canes and [A] silver lanes a[D]glow. [- D7]
[G] It's beginning to look a [C] lot like [G] Christmas, toys in [G7] every [C] store
[C] But the prettiest [A] sight to see is the [G] holly that will [E] be
[Am] On [D] your own front [G] door.
[B7] A pair of hop along boots, and a pistol that shoots,
[Em] Is the wish of Barney and Ben,
[A] Dolls that will talk and will go for a walk,
[D] Is the hope of Janice and [D7] Jen.
[D] And Mom and Dad can [D7] hardly wait for [D] school to start a[D7]gain.

JINGLE BELLS

 G   C
Dashing through the snow in a one-horse open sleigh,
      D7   G
O´er the fields we go, laughing all the way.
 G   C
Bells on bobtail ring, making spirits bright,
       D7   G
What fun it is to ride and sing a sleighing song tonight.
D7 hold
Oh
 G
Jingle bells, jingle bells, jingle all the way,
C   G   A7   D - D7
Oh, what fun it is to run in a one-horse open sleigh, hey
 G
Jingle bells, jingle bells, jingle all the way,
C   G   D7   G
oh, what fun it is to run in a one-horse open sleigh.

 A day or two ago, I thought I`d take a ride,
And soon Miss Fanny Bright was seated by my side.
The horse was lean and lank, misfortune seemed his lot,
We got into a drifted band and we, we got upset.

Jingle bells, jingle bells, jingle all the way,
oh, what fun it is to run in a one-horse open sleigh.
Jingle bells, jingle bells, jingle all the way,
oh, what fun it is to run in a one-horse open sleigh

JINGLE BELL ROCK

   C
Jingle bell, jingle bell, jingle bell rock,
                      G
jingle bells swing and jingle bells ring,
G   G7   G   G7
snowing and blowing up bushels of fun,
G   G7
now the jingle hop has begun.
   C
Jingle bell, jingle bell, jingle bell rock,
                    G
Jingle bells chime in jingle bell time,
  G   G7   G   - G7
Dancing and prancing in Jingle Bell Square
      C
in the frosty air.
    F   Fm   C
What a bright time, it's the right time to rock the night away,
   D   D7   - G   G7
Jingle bell time is a swell time - to go riding in a one-horse sleigh.

Giddy-up jingle horse, pick up your feet, jingle around the clock,
Mix and a-mingle in the jingling feet,   that's the jingle bell rock.

JOLLY OLD ST. NICHOLAS

| G | D | Em | Bm |

Jolly old Saint Nicholas, lean your ear this way,
| C | G | D | D7 |

Don't you tell a single soul what I'm going to say.
| G | D | Em | Bm |

Christmas Eve is coming soon, now, you dear old man,
| C | G | D7 | G |

Whisper what you'll bring to me, tell me if you can.

When the clock is striking twelve, when I'm fast asleep,
down the chimney, broad and black,
With your pack you'll creep.
All the stockings you will find hanging in a row,
mine will be the shortest one, you'll be sure to know.

Johnny wants a pair of skates, Suzy wants a dolly,
Nellie wants a story book, she thinks dolls are folly.
As for me, my little brain isn't very bright,
Choose for me, old Santa Claus,
What you think is right.

JOY TO THE WORLD

   A   E7 A
Joy to the world ! The Lord is come,
      D   E7   A
Let earth receive her King !

Let ev'ry heart, prepare Him room.

And heav'n and nature sing,
    E7
and heav'n and nature sing,
       A   E7   A
And heaven   and heaven and nature sing.

Joy to the earth ! The Savior reigns,
Let men their songs employ !
While fields and floods, rocks, hills, and plains,
Repeat the sounding joy, repeat the sounding joy,
Repeat,   repeat the sounding joy.

He rules the world with truth and grace,
And makes the nations prove,
The glories of His righteousness,
And wonders of His love, and wonders of His love,
And wo...nders, wonde...rs of His love.

O COME ALL YE FAITHFUL

     G   D   G   C G D
O come all ye faithful, joyful and tri - umphant,
  Em D A D   A7 D
O come ye, o come ye to Bethlehem.
  G   D7 G D   Em D
Come on and behold him, born the King of Angels.
  G   D G D
Oh come, let us adore him, oh come, let us adore him,
G D7 G D7 G D7 C G D7 G
O come, let us adore him,   Christ the Lord.

See, how the shepherds, summoned to his cradle,
leaving their flocks draw near with lovely fear.
We will go thither, bend your joyful footsteps.
Oh come, let us adore him, oh come, let us adore him,
o come, let us adore him,   Christ the Lord.

Sing, choirs of angels, sing in exultation,
Sing, all ye citizens of heaven above.
Glory to Go - d, glory in the highest.
Oh come, let us adore him, oh come, let us adore him,
O come, let us adore him,   Christ the Lord.

O HOLY NIGHT

```
   C                F            C
O Holy Night, the stars are brightly shining,
      Am        G            C
It is the night of our dear Savior's birth.
   C                F        C
Long lay the world in sin and error pining,
         Em          B7        Em
Till he appeared and the soul felt it's worth.


     G                  C
 The thrill of hope, the weary world rejoices,
     G              C
for yonder breaks a new and glorious morn.
  Am       Em    Dm        Am
Fall on your knees, o hear the angel voices,
 C - G   C  F    C  -  G                  C
O ni....ght divine,   o night when Christ was born.
 - G   C - F       C        G         C
 O ni.....ght divi....ne, o night,   o night divine.
```

O Holy Night, the stars are brightly shining,
It is the night of our dear Savior's birth.
Long lay the world in sin and error pining,
till he appeared and the soul felt it's worth.

The thrill of hope, the weary world rejoices,
For yonder breaks a new and glorious morn.
Fall on your knees, o hear the angel voices,
Oo ni....ght divine, o night when Christ was born.
O ni.....ght divi....ne, o night,   o night divine.

RUDOLPH THE RED-NOSED REINDEER

     C   Bm   Am   G
You know Dasher, and Dancer, and Prancer, and Vixen,
 C   Bm   Am   G
Comet, and Cupid, and Donner and Blitzen,
 Em   Am   A7   D7
But do you recall the most famous reindeer of all.

 G   D
Rudolph, the red-nosed reindeer had a very shiny nose,
 D   G
And if you ever saw it, you would even say it glows.
 G   D
All of the other reindeer used to laugh and call him names,
 D   G
They never let poor Rudolph join in any reindeer games.
 C   G   C   G
Then one foggy Christmas Eve Santa came to say,
 G   A7   D7
Rudolph with your nose so bright, won't you guide my sleigh tonight?"
 G   D
Then all the reindeer loved him as they shouted out with glee,
 D   G
Rudolph the red-nosed reindeer, you'll go down in history! "

SANTA CLAUS IS COMING TO TOWN

    C   F
You better watch out, you better not cry,
    C   F
You better not pout, I'm telling you why.
C   F   C
 Santa Claus is coming to town,
C   F
Santa Claus is coming to town.
 C   Am   F   - G   C   C G
 Santa Claus is coming   to town.

        C   F
 He's making a list, and checking it twice,
     C   F
He's gonna find out who's naughty and nice
C   F   C
 Santa Claus is coming to town,
C   F
Santa Claus is coming to town.
C   Am   F   - G   C   C G
 Santa Claus is coming   to town.

      C   F
 He sees you when you're sleeping,
    C   F
He knows when you're awake,
    D   G   D   G
He knows if you've been bad or good, so be good for goodness sake!

SILENT NIGHT

```
    G                          D    D7  G
Silent night, holy night! All is calm, all is bright,
   C              G
Round yon Virgin, Mother and Child,
   C         G
Holy infant so tender and mild,
    D     D7      G - Em    G     D7       G
Sleep in heavenly   peace, sleep in heavenly
peace.
```

Silent night, holy night! Shepherds quake at the sight,
Glories stream from heaven afar,
Heavenly hosts sing Alleluia,
Christ the Savior is born! Christ the Savior is born!

 Silent night, holy night! Son of God love's pure light,
Radiant beams from Thy holy face,
Wwith the dawn of redeeming grace,
Jesus Lord, at Thy   birth, Jesus Lord, at Thy birth.

SILVER BELLS

[G] [C]
Silver bells, silver bells,
[D]   [D7]   [G] -
It's Christmas time in the city
[G] [C]
Ring-a-ling hear them ring (
[D]   [D7]   [G]
Soon it will be Christmas day.

[G]   [C]   (Am)
City sidewalks, busy sidewalks dressed in holiday style,
[D]   [D7]   [G]   - D
In the air there's a feeling of Christmas.
[G]   [C]   (Am)
Children laughing, people passing, meeting smile after smile,
[D]   [D7]   [G]
And on ev'ry street corner you hear :
CHORUS

Strings of street lights, even stop lights blink a bright red and green,
As the shoppers rush home with their treasures.
Hear the snow crunch, see the kids bunch, this is
Santa's big scene, and above all this bustle you hear :

SIX WHITE BOOMERS

In Australia Christmas comes in the middle of a very hot summer, so when Santa Claus delivers his presents he is not taken round by reindeer because they can't stand the terrible heat. He's taken round by six big wild old men kangaroos called the "Six White Boomers.

```
  G                              C         G
Early on one Christmas Day, a Joey Kangaroo
                        Em        A      D
Was far from home and lost in a great big zoo.
  G               G7            C         G
Mummy, where's my mummy, they've taken her away
   - - - - - - - - - - - - - - - - - - (D7) - - - - (G)   - G - C - G
We'll help you find your mummy, son, hop on the sleigh!
```

Up beside the bag of toys, little Joey hopped,
But they hadn't gone far when Santa stopped.
Unharnessed all the reindeer and Joey wondered why,
then he heard a far off booming in the sky.
   (make boom" noises)

```
  G       G7       C         G
Six white boomers, snow white boomers,
                Em            A      D
racing Santa Claus through the blazing sun.
  G       G7       C       G
Six white boomers, snow white boomers,
  G - - - - - - - - D    G
 on his Australian run.
```

THE FIRST NOEL

      G   C   G
The first Noel the angels did say
     C   C   D7 G
was to certain poor shephards in fields where they lay.
    G   C   G
In fi…elds where they lay keeping their sheep
     C   G   D7 G
On a cold winter's night that was so deep.
 G   C   G   D7 G
Noel, Noel, Noel, Noel, born is the King of Isael.

They lookéd up and saw a star,
shining in the east beyond them far.
And to the earth it gave great light,
and so it continued both day and night.
Noel, Noel, Noel, Noel, born is the King of Israel.

And by the light of that same star,
three wise men came from country far.
To seek for a King was their intent,
and to follow the st.ar wherever it went.
Noel, Noel, Noel, Noel,
born is the King of Israel.

THE LTTLE DRUMMER BOY

```
    C              F    C
Come , they told me, parapapompom,
                        F     C
a newborn king to see, parapapompom,
G        C                  G
our finest gifts we bring, parapapompom,
G7        C         F
to set before the king, parapapompom,
  C         G
rapapompom, rapapompom.
 C              F       C      G       C
So to honour him, parapapompom, when we come.
```

Little Baby, parapapompom,
I am a poor boy, too, parapapompom,
I have no gift to bring, parapapompom,
that`s fit to give a king, parapapompom,
rapapompom, rapapompom.
Shall I play for you, parapapompom, on my drum.

Then he nodded, parapapompom,
the ox and lamb kept time, parapapompom,
I played my drum for him, parapapompom,
I played my best for him, parapapompom,
rapapompom, rapapompom.
Then he smiled at me, parapapompom, me and my drum,
```
 G       C  G      C  G        C
me and my drum, me and my drum, me and my drum.
```

THE 12 DAYS OF CHRISTMAS

      C   G   C
On the first day of Christmas my true love gave to me
  C F   C   G C
a partridge in a pear tree.
      C   G   C
On the second day of Christmas my true love gave to me :
G
two turtle doves,
  C F   C   G C
and a partridge in a pear tree.
      C   G   C
On the third day of Christmas my true love gave to me
G
three French hens, two turtle doves,
  C F   C   G C
and a partridge in a pear tree.
      C   G   C
On the fourth day of Christmas my true love gave to me
G
four calling birds, three French hens, two turtle doves,
  C F   C   G C
and a partridge in a pear tree.
      C   G   C
On the fifth day of Christmas my true love gave to me :
Em D   G
five golden rings.

```
    C            F          G
 Four calling birds, three French hens, two turtle doves,
       C F    C   G   C
 and a partridge in a pear tree.
              C                    G           C
 On the sixth day of Christmas my true love gave to me :
 G              Em   D     G
 six geese-a-laying, five golden rings
    C            F          G
 Four calling birds, three French hens, two turtle doves,
       C F    C   G   C
 and a partridge in a pear tree.
                C                          G             C
 On the seventh day of Christmas my true love gave to me
   G
 seven swans-a-swimming, six geese-a-laying,
 Em  D     G
 five golden rings.
    C            F          G
 Four calling birds, three French hens, two turtle doves,
       C F    C   G   C
 and a partridge in a pear tree.
                C                     G          C
 On the eigth day of Christmas my true love gave to me
   G
 eight maids-a-milking, seven swans-a-swimming, six geese-a-laying,
 Em  D     G
 five golden rings.
    C            F          G
 Four calling birds, three French hens, two turtle doves,
```

      C F   C   G   C
and a partridge in a pear tree.
       C   G   C
On the ninth day of Christmas my true love gave to me:
G
nine ladies dancing, eight maids-a-milking, seven swans-a-swimming,
G   Em   D   G
six geese-a-laying, five golden rings
 C   F   G
Four calling birds, three French hens, two turtle doves,
     C F   C   G   C
and a partridge in a pear tree.
        C   G   C
On the tenth day of Christmas my true love gave to me
 G
ten lords-a-leaping, nine ladies dancing, eight maids-a-milking,
G
seven swans-a-swimming, six geese-a-laying,
Em D   G
five golden rings.
   C   F   G
Four calling birds, three French hens, two turtle doves,
     C F   C   G   C
and a partridge in a pear tree.

         C   G   C
On the eleventh day of Christmas my true love gave to me :
 G

eleven pipers piping, ten lords-a-leaping, nine ladies dancing,
  G

eight maids-a-milking, seven swans-a-swimming, six geese-a-laying,
Em D   G

five golden rings.
  C   F   G

Four calling birds, three French hens, two turtle doves,
      C F   C   G   C

and a partridge in a pear tree.
        C   G   C

On the twelfth day of Christmas my true love gave to me :
  G

twelve drummers drumming, eleven pipers piping, ten lords-a-leaping,
  G

nine ladies dancing, eight maids-a-milking, seven swans-a-swimming,
  G

six geese-a-laying,
Em D   G

five golden rings.
  C   F   G

Four calling birds, three French hens, two turtle doves,
      C F   C   G   C

WE THREE KINGS OF ORIENT ARE

Em   B7 Em
We three kings of Orient are,
             B7   Em
Bearing gifts we traverse afar,
         D   G   C
Ffield and fountain, moor and mountain,
Am   Em B7   Em
Following yonder star.

D - D7   G   C   G
O.......o ! Star of wonder, star of night,
              C   G
Star with royal beauty bright,
Em   D G C   D   G
Westward leading still proceeding,
G   C   G
Guide us to thy perfect light !

Born a king on Bethlehem's plain, gold I bring to crown him again,
 King forever, ceasing never, over us all to reign.
CHORUS

Frankincense to offer have I, incense owns a deity neigh.
 Prayer and praising, all men raising, worship Him, God most high.
CHORUS

WE WISH YOU A MERRY CHRISTMAS

     G   C
We wish you a merry Christmas,
   Am   D
We wish you a merry Christmas,
   Bm   Em   C   D   G
We wish you a merry Christmas and a happy new year.
    G   D   Em   D7
Good tidings we bring to you and your kin,
    G   D   Am D7 G
We wish you a merry Christmas and a happy new year.

Now bring us the figgy pudding,
Now bring us the figgy pudding,
Nnow bring us the figgy pudding,
And bring some out here. + CHORUS

For we all like the figgy pudding,
For we all like the figgy pudding,
For we all like the figgy pudding,
So bring some out here. + CHORUS

And we won`t go until we`ve got some,
And we won`t go until we`ve got one,
And we won`t go until we`ve got some,
So bring some out here. + CHORUS

WHITE CHRISTMAS

G   Am   D
I`m dreaming of a white Christmas
C   D   G
Just like the ones I used to know
                      G7   C   Am
Where the tree tops glisten und children listen
  G Em   Am - D
To hear bells sound in the snow

I`m dreaming of a white Christmas
With every Christmas card I write.
 May your days be merry and bright -
And may all your Christmasses be white.

THE CHRISTMAS SONG

```
   C – Fm – F – G     C – Fm – F – G
C           Dm        C        - Dm
```
Chestnuts roasting on an open fire,
```
C           Gm        F     - Fm
```
Jack Frost nipping at your nose.
```
Am       Fm         C        B7
```
Yuletide carols being sung by a choir,
```
E         Fm             Dm  - G
```
 and folks dressed up like Eskimos.

Everybody knows a turkey and some mistletoe,
   help to make the season bright.
   Tiny tots with their eyes all a-glow,
```
     Em   Dm      F    G  C
```
   will find it hard to sleep tonight.
```
                Gm  - C     Gm  - C
```
 They know that Santa's   on his way,
```
             Gm     C                  F
```
he's loaded lots of toys and goodies on his sleigh.
```
     Fm        - Bb      Eb
```
And ev'ry mother's child   is gonna spy,
```
     Am    - D               F  - G7
```
to see if reindeer   really know how to fly.

And so, I'm offering this simple phrase,
   to kids from one to ninety-two,
   although it's been said many times, many ways,
   "Merry Christmas   to you!"

SLEIGHRIDE

```
            C         Am
Just hear those sleigh bells jingle-ing,
Dm      G    C
ring ting tingle-ing too,
   G      C      Am
come on, it's lovely weather
      Dm       G        C
for a sleigh ride together with you !
   G      C  - Am
Outside the snow is falling,
  Dm       G       C
and friends are calling "You Hoo" !
   G    C       Am
Come on, it's lovely weather
      Dm      G       C
for a sleigh ride together with you.


   F#m       - B                     E
 Giddy-yap giddy-yap, giddy-yap let's go,    let's look
at the snow,
  F3m              B         E
 we're riding in wonderland of snow.
    Em            A              D
 Giddy-yap giddy-yap, giddy-yap it's grand,   just
holding your hand,
Dm                                  G
we're gliding along with the song of a wintry fairy land.
```

ROCKIN' AROUND THE CHRISTMAS TREE

```
 C                             G
Rockin' around the Christmas tree at the Christmas
Party Hop,
 G7                           G         C
Mistletoe hung where you can see every couple tries
to stop.
                              G
Rockin' around the Christmas tree, let the Christmas
spirit ring,
G7                            G         C
later we'll have some pumpkin pie, and we'll do some
carolling.

 F              Em
You will get a sentimental feeling when you hear
 Am       D7        G           G7
voices singing, let's be jolly, deck the halls with
boughs of holly !
```

Rockin' around the Christmas tree, have a happy holiday, everyone dancin' merrily in the new old fashioned way.

You will get a sentimental feeling when you hear voices singing, let's be jolly, deck the halls with boughs of holly !
Rockin' around the Christmas tree, have a happy holiday, everyone dancin' merrily in the new old fashioned way.

OH LITTLE TOWN OF BETHLEHEM

G 　　C　　　　　　G　　D　　　G
Oh little town of Bethlehem, how still we see thee lie,
　　　　E7　　　Am　　　　　　G　　D7　G
above thy deep and dreamless sleep the silent stars go by.
Em　　　　　　B7　　　　Em　　　　B7
Yet in thy dark streets shineth, the everlasting light.
　G　　　　　　C　　　　　　G　　D7　G
The hopes and fears of all the years are met in thee tonight.

For Christ is born of Mary, and gathered all above
While mortals sleep the angels keep their watch of wondering love.
Oh morning stars together, proclaim thy holy birth.
And praises sing to God the king, and peace to men on earth.

Oh little town of Bethlehem, how still we see thee lie,
above thy deep and dreamless sleep the silent stars go by.
Yet in thy dark streets shineth, the everlasting light.
The hopes and fears of all the years are met in thee tonight.

FROSTY THE SNOWMAN

G
Thumpety thump thump, thumpety thump thump,
           D7
Look at Frosty go.

Thumpety thump thump, thumpety thump thump,
                                    G
Over the hills of snow...Oh...Oh...over the hills of snow.

G   C   G
Frosty the Snow Man, was a jolly happy soul
   C   G
With a corn-cob pipe and a button nose
      D   G
And two eyes made out of coal.
G   C   G
Frosty the Snow Man, is a fairy tale they say
   C   G
He was made of snow but the children know
  C   D7   G
How he came to life one day.

   C   Bm   Am   G
There must have been some magic in that old silk hat they found,
   D   Dbdim   Em   D
For when they put it on his head he began to dance around.

Oh, Frosty the Snow Man was alive as he could be,
And the children say he could laugh and play

just the same as you and me.

Frosty the Snow Man,' knew the sun was hot that day,
So he said, "Let's run and we'll have some fun
now before I melt away."

Down to the village, with a broomstick in his hand,
Running here and there all around the square,
saying "Catch me if you can."

   C   Bm   Am   G
He led them down the streets of town right to the traffic cop,
    D   Dbdim   Em   D
And he only paused a moment when he heard him holler, "Stop!"

Frosty the Snow Man had to hurry on his way,
But he waved good-bye, saying, "Don't you cry;
I'll be back again some day."

[Ending]
G
Thumpety thump thump, thumpety thump thump,
       D7
Look at Frosty go.

Thumpety thump thump, thumpety thump thump,
                     G
over the hills of snow...Oh...Oh...over the hills of snow

ALPHABETICAL LISTING

TITLE	PAGE
A Hard Rains Gonna Fall	75
A Worried Man	167
ABBA	**63**
Abilene	121
Act Naturally	122
All American Boy	281
All I Have o Do Is Dream	257
All I have to Do is Dream	36
Alley Opp	243
Amanda	123
American Pie	288
Annie's Song	55
Annies Song	28
Are You Lonesome Tonight	219
Bad Bad Leroy Brown	255
Ballad Of A Teenage Queen	108
Be Bop A Lula	259
Big Bad John	190
Big Iron	49
Big River	105
Black Fly	152
Blow Ye winds	176
Blowin In The Wind	70
Blue Suede Shoes	270
BOB DYLAN	**69**
Bobby McGee	132
BONEY M	**91**
Book Of Love	250

Book Of Love	279
Bottle Of Wine	197
Boy Named Sue	106
Brown Girl In The Ring	94
Bye Bye Love	258
Calypso	59
CARIBBEAN BEAT	**154**
Cecilia	41
Chantilly Lace	271
City of New Orleans	12
Closing Time	182
Cockles and Mussels	84
Colors	239
Cool Water	205
Coplas Revisited	170
Cotton Fields Back Home	31
Country Roads	27
Country Roads	54
Craklin Rosie	98
Cry Of The wild Goose	206
Daddy Sang Bass	118
Danny Boy	85
Delilah	22
Della And The Dealer	145
Delta Dawn	224
Devil Woman	52
Don`t Take Your Love To Town	130
Don't Think Twice	71
DONOVAN	**235**
Down By The Station	252

Downtown	284
Drunken Sailor	178
Durham Town	79
Eagle	67
Eidleweiss	38
El Matador	169
El Paso	48
England Swings	192
Everglades	168
Everybody Knows	185
Farewell Adelita	160
Fast Freight	230
Five Feet High and Risen	109
Five Hundred Miles	21
Folsom Prison Blues	116
For Baby	56
Four Strong Winds	23
Frankie And Johny	198
Froggie went A Courtin	196
Frosty The Snowman	321
Get Rhythm	112
Ghost Riders	26
God Rest ye Merry Gentelmen	290
Good to be back Home Again	57
Good King Wenseslas	291
Gotta Travel On	76
Grammas Feather Bed	61
Grandfathers Clock	215
Green Fields	17
Green Green	20

Green Green Grass of Home	58
Greenback Dollar	164
Greensleeves	18
Guantanamera	45
Guess Things Happen That Way	113
Hakuna Matata	208
Hark the Herald Angels Sing	292
Hava Nagilh	29
Have I Told You Lately That I Love You	125
Have Yourself a Merry Little Christmas	293
Heart Aches by the Number	126
Heartbreak Hotel	200
Here Comes Santa Claus	295
Hi Lili Lili Lo	171
High Hopes	233
Home Of The Blues	107
Honeycomb	256
Hound Dog	273
House of the Rising Sun	11
Hurdy Gurdy Man	240
I Can See Clearly	191
I Don't Have a Wooden Heart	35
I Have A dream	64
I Kissed Ya	260
I Like Beer	228
I Walk The Line	119
I Wanna Go Home	159
I`d Like To Teach The world To Sing	177
I'll See You in my Dreams	46
If I Were A Rich Man	211

IRISH MELODIES 83

It Ai'nt Me Babe	74
It Came Upon a Midnight Clear	294
It`s A Heartache	148
Its Beginning to look a lot like Xmas	296
Its So Easy	265
Itsy Bitsy Bikini	246
Jackson	204
Jailhouse Rock	275
Jamaica Farewell	156
Jambalaya	127
Jennifer Juniper	236
Jesse James	187
Jingle Bell Rock	298
Jingle Bells	297

JOHN DENVER 53
JOHNNY CASH 104

Johny B Goode	276
Jolly old St Nicolas	299
Jonny Is A Joker	261
Joy To The world	153
Joy to the World	300
Just An Old Hippy	140
Just walking In The Rain	199
Kalinka	44

KENNY ROGERS 99

King Of The Road	133

KINGSTON TRIO 161

Kiss An Angel Good Morning	128

Kisses Sweeter Than Wine	253
Kokomo	286
La Bamba	157
Lemon Tree	217
LEONARD COHEN	**179**
Let Me Be There	141
Look what They`ve Done To My Song	285
Love is Blue	19
Love Is Blue	78
Love Potion Number 9	277
Lucille	102
Luckenbach Texas	129
Margaritaville	225
Marianne	158
MARTY ROBBINS	**47**
Mellow Yellow	232
Michael Row The Boat Ashore	203
Monster Mash	242
Morning has Broken	13
Mr Tamborine Man	72
Mrs. Robinson	189
My Lover was a Logger (Logger Love)	188
NEIL DIAMOND	**95**
Never Ending Song of Love	43
Never On Sunday	34
New World In the Morning	80
NICE MELODIES	**10**
North To Alaska	223
O come all Ye Faithfull	301
O Holy night	302

O Little Town of Bethlehem	320
Oakie From Muskogee	131
Ob La Di	42
OH Lord It's Hard to Be Humble	135
Oh My Darling Clemintine	214
OLD FAVORITES	**186**
OLD FUNNIES	**241**
Old Toy trains	30
On The Road Again	124
Only The Lonely	278
Party Doll	251
Peggy Sue	266
Puff the Magic Dragon	24
Purple People Eater	244
Put Another Log On The Fire	136
Raindrops Keep Falling On My Head	231
Raspberries Strawberries	172
Rasputin	92
Rave On	267
Rhinestone Cowboy	142
Ring Of Fire	115
River Lady	82
Rivers Of Babylon	93
ROCKIN & ROLLIN	**248**
Rockin Around the Christmas Tree	319
ROGER WHITTACKER	**77**
Roving Gambler	174
Rudolf the red nosed reindeer	303
Rueben James	103
Rueben James	165

Running Bear	193
Running Gun	50
Santa claus is coming to town	304
Save The Last Dance For Me	280
Scarborough Fair	15
Shenandoah	138
Silent Night	305
Silver Bells	306
Silver Threads And Golden Needles	149
Singin The Blues	254
Singing The Blues	274
Sinking Of The Reuben James	173
Six White Boomers	307
Sixteen Tons	134
Sleighride	318
Sloop John B	155
Sneaky Snake	227
Song Sung Blue	96
Sound of Silence	16
Squaws Along The Yukon	194
Star Of The County Down	86
Stewball	221
Storms Never Last	139
Summer Wages	144
Sundown	137
Sweet Caroline	97
Sweet Georgia Brown	249
Take A Chance On Me	65
Take This Waltz	181
Taken`Care Of Business	287

Tennessee Flat Top Box	117
Tennessee Stud	114
Thank God I'm a Country Boy	60
That'll Be The Day	268
The Battle Of New Orleans	201
The Christmas Song	317
The Erie Canal	175
The First Noel	308
The Future	180
The Gambler	100
The Hanging Tree	51
The Happy Wanderer	210
The Last Farwell	81
The Little Drummer Boy	309
The MTA	163
The Night They Drove old Dixie	62
The Piper	68
The Reverend Mr Black	207
The Singing Nun	37
The Unicorn Song	90
There is a Tavern in this Town	88
This Land Is Your Land	218
Those were the Days my Friend	14
Three wheels On My Wagon	151
Thunder Road	229
Tie Me Kangaroo Down Sport	247
Tijuana Jail	166
Times They are A Changin	73
Tom Dooley	162
Try To Remember	283

Twelve Days of Xmas	310
Universal Soldier	237
Vaya Codios	213
Wabash Cannonball	202
Wake Up Little Susie	262
Walk On By	143
Walk Right In	222
Waltzing Matilda	220
Watermelon Wine	226
We Three Kings of Orient are	314
We Wish you a Merry Christmas	315
Well Alright	269
WESTERN COUNTRY MIX	**120**
When The Saints Go Marchin In	216
Where have all the flowers Gone	25
Whiskey In The Jar	87
White Christmas	316
White Lightening	272
Who's Sorry Now	39
Wild Colonial Boy	89
Wildwood Flower	32
Wings Of A Dove	195
Witch Doctor	245
Wolverton Mountain	146
XMAS FAVORITES	**289**
Yellow Bird	33
Young Love	263
Young Love 2	264

BANJO CHORDS G TUNING

CHORDS IN G TUNING

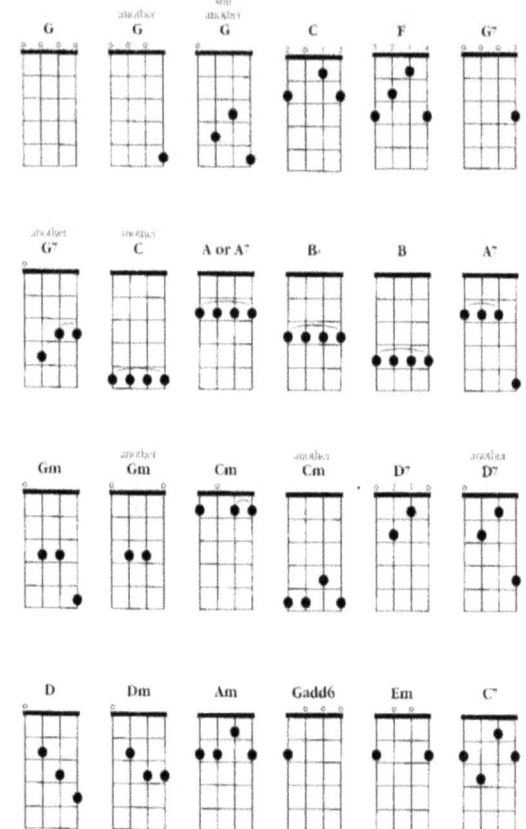

BANJO CHORDS C TUNING

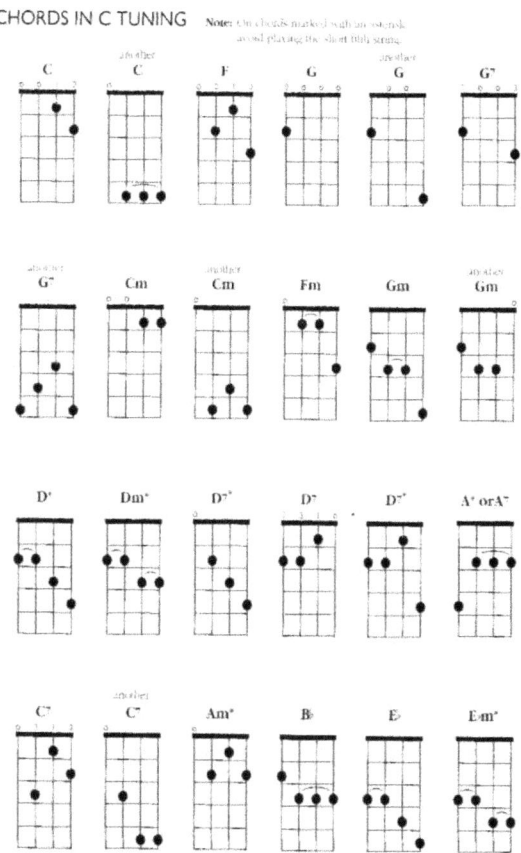

GUITAR CHORDS

GUITAR CHORD CHART

	MAJOR	MINOR	MAJ. 6th	MIN. 6th	DOM. 7th	MAJ. 7th	AUG. 7th	MIN. 7th	AUG. (+)	DIM. (0)
C	C	Cm	C6	Cm6	C7	Cmaj7	C7+5	Cm7	C+	Cdim
Db or C#	Db	Dbm	Db6	Dbm6	Db7	Dbmaj7	Db7+5	Dbm7	Db+	Dbdim
D	D	Dm	D6	Dm6	D7	Dmaj7	D7+5	Dm7	D+	Ddim
Eb	Eb	Ebm	Eb6	Ebm6	Eb7	Ebmaj7	Eb7+5	Ebm7	Eb+	Ebdim
E	E	Em	E6	Em6	E7	Emaj7	E7+5	Em7	E+	Edim
F	F	Fm	F6	Fm6	F7	Fmaj7	F7+5	Fm7	F+	Fdim
Gb or F#	Gb	Gbm	Gb6	Gbm6	Gb7	Gbmaj7	Gb7+5	Gbm7	Gb+	Gbdim
G	G	Gm	G6	Gm6	G7	Gmaj7	G7+5	Gm7	G+	Gdim
Ab	Ab	Abm	Ab6	Abm6	Ab7	Abmaj7	Ab7+5	Abm7	Ab+	Abdim
A	A	Am	A6	Am6	A7	Amaj7	A7+5	Am7	A+	Adim
Bb	Bb	Bbm	Bb6	Bbm6	Bb7	Bbmaj7	Bb7+5	Bbm7	Bb+	Bbdim
B	B	Bm	B6	Bm6	B7	Bmaj7	B7+5	Bm7	B+	Bdim

www.ingramcontent.com/pod-product-compliance
Lightning Source LLC
Chambersburg PA
CBHW070614160426
43194CB00009B/1265